Cultural Hybridity

Cultural Hybridity

PETER BURKE

polity

First published in 2009 by Polity Press

Polity Press
65 Bridge Street
Cambridge CB2 1UR, UK

Polity Press
350 Main Street
Malden, MA 02148, USA

ISBN-13: 978-0-7456-4696-1
ISBN-13: 978-0-7456-4697-8 (paperback)

A catalogue record for this book is available from the British Library.

Book designed and typeset in 11 on 15pt Adobe Garamond
by Peter Ducker MISTD

Printed and bound in Great Britain
by MPG Books Limited, Bodmin, Cornwall

The publisher has used its best endeavours to ensure that the URLs for external
websites referred to in this book are correct and active at the time of going to
press. However, the publisher has no responsibility for the websites and can
make no guarantee that a site will remain live or that the content is or will
remain appropriate.

Every effort has been made to trace all copyright holders, but if any have been
inadvertently overlooked the publishers will be pleased to include any necessary
credits in any subsequent reprint or edition.

For further information on Polity, visit our website: www.politybooks.com.

For Marco and Lara
Multi-cultural children

'All cultures are the result of a mishmash'
(Claude Lévi-Strauss)

'The history of all cultures is the history of
cultural borrowing'
(Edward Said)

'Today, all cultures are frontier cultures'
(Nestor Canclini)

CONTENTS

This brief essay on an extensive subject has a complicated international history. In 1999 the Einstein Forum invited me to give a lecture in Berlin on a topic of contemporary relevance and I chose 'cultural exchange': the following year Suhrkampf Verlag of Frankfurt published a German translation of the lecture under the title *Kultureller Austausch*. A couple of years later a Brazilian publisher, Editora Unisinos of São Leopoldo, invited me to write a short book for a series of theirs, so I revised the Berlin lecture and expanded it from about thirty pages to about a hundred, adding a number of Brazilian examples. This Brazilian version, *Hibridismo cultural*, appeared in 2003.

More recently, Ediciones Akal suggested a Spanish translation, and I took advantage of this opportunity to expand the essay a little more, as well as to update the references. An Italian publisher, QuiEdit of Verona, then expressed interest, and I thought that this might also be the time for an English version to appear, once again expanded. It now weighs in at over 130 pages.

I have learned a good deal in the course of these

attempts to revise and expand what was originally a lecture, as well as to communicate with German, Brazilian, Spanish, Italian and Anglophone readers and to find examples relevant to their different experiences. One might say that cultural globalization, a theme that is naturally discussed in the essay itself, has made its impact (if not had its revenge) on the author.

A recent discussion of post-modernity, by the British historian Perry Anderson, describes the tendency of the period we live in to celebrate the 'cross-over, the hybrid, the pot-pourri'.[1] More exactly, some people – like the Anglo-Indian writer Salman Rushdie, especially in his *Satanic Verses* (1988) – celebrate these phenomena, while others fear or condemn them. The condemnations are issued, it should be added, from very different political positions, since the critics of hybridity include Muslim fundamentalists, white segregationists and black separatists. The conceptual problems raised by the employment of the term 'hybridity', which has been described as 'maddeningly elastic', will be discussed in chapter 2 below.[2]

One sign of the intellectual climate of our age is the growing use of the term 'essentialism' as a way of criticizing one's opponent in many kinds of argument. Nations, social classes, tribes and castes have all been 'deconstructed' in the sense of being described as false entities. An unusually sophisticated example of the trend is a book by a French anthropologist, Jean-Loup Amselle, called *Logiques métisses* (1990). Amselle, a specialist on West Africa, argues that there is no such thing as a tribe such as the Fulani or the Bambara. There is no sharp or firm cultural frontier between groups, but rather a cultural continuum.[3] Linguists have long been making a similar point about neighbouring languages such as Dutch and German. On the frontier, it is impossible to say exactly when or where Dutch stops and German begins.

A preoccupation with the topic is natural in a period like ours that is marked by increasingly frequent and intense cultural encounters of all kinds. The consequences of cultural globalization are debatable and debated. One possibility, to be discussed below, is cultural homogenization, while some scholars suggest the opposite, heterogenization. Whatever the merits of these arguments, especially where long-term consequences are concerned, it is difficult to deny that what we see, hear and experience in other ways in the short term is some kind of mix, a process of hybridization that assists economic globalization as well as being assisted by it.[4]

However we react to it, this global trend is impossible to miss, from curry and chips – recently voted the favourite dish in Britain – to Thai saunas, Zen Catholicism or Judaism, Nigerian Kung Fu, or 'Bollywood' films, made in Bombay-Mumbai and mixing Indian traditions of song and dance with the conventions of Hollywood. This process is particularly obvious in the domain of music, in the case of such hybrid forms and genres as jazz, reggae, salsa or, more recently, flamenco rock and Afro-Celtic rock. New technology – including, appropriately enough, the 'mixer' - has obviously facilitated this kind of hybridization.[5]

No wonder, then, that a group of theorists of hybridity have made their appearance, themselves often of double or mixed cultural identity. Homi Bhabha (1949–) for instance, is an Indian who has taught in England and now lives in the USA. Stuart Hall (1932–) who was born in Jamaica of mixed parentage, has lived most of his life in England and describes himself as 'a mongrel culturally, the absolute cultural hybrid'.[6] Paul Gilroy (1956–), also of mixed parentage, was born in London and has worked in the USA. Ien Ang describes herself as 'an ethnic Chinese, Indonesian-born and European-educated academic who now lives and works in Australia'.[7] On the other hand, the late Edward Said (1935–2003), a Palestinian who grew up in Egypt and taught in the USA, described himself as 'out of place' wherever he was located (in similar fashion, Jawaharlal Nehru, the first Prime Minister of India after its independence, once declared that he had become 'a queer mixture of the East and West, out of place everywhere').[8]

Compared to these individuals, the sociologist Nestor García Canclini (1939–), who grew up in Argentina but works in Mexico, and the anthropologist Eduardo Archetti (1943–2005), an Argentinian who moved to Norway, may hardly seem to be mixtures at all. All the same, their personal experience of life in different cultures, or living between different cultures, surely underlies their concern with questions of hybridity.[9]

Indeed, Latin America has seemed to many people to be the hybrid region *par excellence*, since it has been the site of encounters, clashes, miscegenation and other interactions between the indigenous population, the European invaders, and the slaves whom the Europeans brought from Africa. Hybridity was celebrated by the Mexican José Vasconcelos (1881–1959), the Minister of Education and author of *The Cosmic Race* (1929), which presented the mestizo as the essence of the Mexican nation, and by the Brazilian sociologist-historian Gilberto Freyre (1900-87), whose *Masters and the Slaves* (1933) defined the identity of Brazilians in terms of mixing, especially between European and African cultures.[10]

Writers who employ the concept have also been faulted for identifying Latin American culture with hybridity and so blurring distinctions between different regions of Latin America. Uruguay, for instance, with a population that is mainly of Spanish and Italian descent, is very different

4

from its neighbour Brazil, where Africans, Japanese, and immigrants from many parts of Europe, as well as the indigenous population, have contributed to the cultural mix.[11]

The work of the theorists mentioned above has attracted growing interest in a number of disciplines, from anthropology to literature, from geography to art history, and from musicology to religious studies, although workers in one discipline are not always aware of what is happening in some of the others. Historians too are devoting increasing attention to the processes of cultural encounter, contact, interaction, exchange and hybridization, as the notes to this volume will show.

The text that you are now reading, however, is not, or not only, a study of cultural history but an essay that is as hybrid as its subject, concerned with the present as well as the past, with theories as well as practices, and with general processes as well as specific events. Although processes of hybridization may be found in the economic, social and political spheres, this essay will confine itself to cultural trends, defining the term 'culture' in a reasonably broad sense to include attitudes, mentalities and values and their expression, embodiment or symbolization in artefacts, practices and representations.

In an informal, personal essay of this kind it is best to state one's own position right at the start. Let me therefore explain that, as a northern European who has always been attracted to Latin cultures (from Spain to Brazil), as well as a Westerner fascinated by what Europeans used to call the 'Middle' and 'Far' East, my own experience of cultural interaction (whether between individuals, disciplines or cultures) has been extremely positive. In any case, the argument that all innovation is a kind of adaptation and that cultural encounters encourage creativity is one that I find extremely plausible.

All the same, I did not write this essay in order to celebrate cultural exchanges or cultural hybridity but in order to analyse these phenomena. In the analysis that follows, I shall try to be as detached as possible. Detached, not objective, since it is impossible to escape from one's own position in history and society. I firmly believe in the value of standing back, at least temporarily, from one's own situation, and so taking a longer and wider view than is possible in other circumstances. This is the distinctively academic contribution – and one that is especially appropriate for a cultural historian – to a debate that concerns most of us today.

In this particular case, I have no wish to present cultural exchange as simple enrichment, forgetting that it sometimes takes place at someone's expense – sometimes quite literally. For example, in the field of music, especially popular music, Westerners have borrowed from other cultures, among them the Pygmies of Central Africa, copyrighting the result without sharing their royalties with the original musicians. In other words, they have treated Third World music as a kind of raw material that is 'processed' in Europe or North America.[12] In similar fashion, over the last 500 years or so, Western scholars have often exploited indigenous knowledge of plants, healing and so on in different parts of the world and they have not always acknowledged their sources.[13]

The concept of hybridity has also been criticized for offering 'a harmonious image of what is obviously disjointed and confrontational' and for ignoring cultural and social discrimination.[14] It is obvious enough that prolonged encounters between human groups have included a good deal of conflict. However, it may be useful to distinguish these social conflicts from their unintended consequences over the long term – the mixture, interpenetration or hybridization of cultures. African music, for example, travels the world with less difficulty than Africans.

The price of hybridization, especially the unusually rapid hybridization that is characteristic of our time, also includes the loss of regional traditions and of local roots. It is surely no accident that the present age of cultural globalization, sometimes viewed more superficially as 'Americanization', is also the age of reactive nationalisms or ethnicities – Serb and Croat, Tutsi and Hutu, Arab and Israeli, Basque and Catalan, and so on. Freyre famously celebrated both regionalism and what he called the 'interpenetration' of cultures, but there is usually a tension between them.

Freyre was one of the first scholars anywhere to devote as much attention to cultural hybridity as he did in 1933 in his study of the masters and the slaves in the sugar plantations of Northeastern Brazil, *Casa Grande e Senzala*.[15] In similar fashion, still in the 1930s, the North American anthropologist Melville Herskovits (1895–1963), who worked on Haiti, discussed what he called the syncretizing of African gods and Catholic saints in the New World.[16] A little later, the sociologist Fernando Ortiz (1881–1969) and the novelist-musicologist Alejo Carpentier y Valmont (1904–80) made similar points about Cuba.[17]

In the case of Europe, two studies of the 1930s and 1940s stand out in this respect. *The Making of Europe* (1932), by the English cultural historian Christopher Dawson (1889–1970), focussed on the period 500–1000 and emphasized three contributions: those of the classical, Christian and 'barbarian' traditions. Although Dawson did not use terms such as 'hybridity', the book may be viewed retrospectively as a study in cultural contact, interaction and hybridization. Again, Américo

Castro y Quesada (1885–1972) offered a controversial interpretation of Spanish history that privileged the encounters and interactions between three cultures: the Christian, the Jewish and the Muslim. Only recently has this idea become widely accepted in Spain.[18]

In the 1950s, the British historian Arnold Toynbee reflected on what he was already calling 'encounters' between cultures, on the importance of diasporas and on the nature of cultural 'reception'.[19] He devoted two volumes of his multi-volume *Study of History* (1934–61) to what he called 'contacts between civilizations' in space and time, 'colliding cultures', or the 'diffraction' of 'culture-rays'.[20] Unlike most Englishmen of his generation, Toynbee was attracted to a kind of religious syncretism. He even recorded a religious experience in the National Gallery in London in 1951 in which he invoked Buddha, Muhammad and 'Christ Tammuz, Christ Adonis, Christ Osiris'.[21]

Some people, whom we might describe as 'purists', were deeply shocked by the arguments of Freyre, Castro and Toynbee when they were first published. Today, by contrast, many of us are prepared to find hybridization almost everywhere in history. In an age of cultural globalization – even if the strength of this movement is sometimes exaggerated – historians are increasingly sensitized to similar phenomena in the past.

Historians of the ancient world, for example, such as

Arnaldo Momigliano (1908–87), have become more and more interested in the process of 'Hellenization', which they are coming to view less as a simple imposition of Greek culture on the Roman Empire and more in terms of interaction between a centre and a periphery.[22] The idea of 'syncretism', launched by the Belgian Franz Cumont (1868–1947), from which a later generation of scholars distanced themselves, is coming back into favour.[23] Again, historians of the Renaissance have become more concerned than they used to be with the Byzantine, Jewish and Muslim contributions to that movement, rather than treating it as a spontaneously generated Italian or Western European 'miracle'.[24]

In an age of an increasingly ecumenical Christianity, historians of the Reformation are more willing today than they once were to admit the importance of cultural exchanges between Catholics and Protestants. For example, the devotional writings of Counter-Reformation Catholics, such as the Spaniard Luis de Granada, the Italian Lorenzo Scupoli and the Frenchman Saint François de Sales were translated into English and were read with approval by Protestants, among them the poets George Herbert and Andrew Marvell, while John Wesley himself, the founder of Methodism, recommended works by Pascal and Fénelon.[25]

Again, some historians of the European missions to

Asia, Africa and America claim that the 'converts' did not so much abandon their traditional religions for Christianity as make some kind of synthesis between them.[26] Sometimes the mixture was obvious to the missionaries themselves, as in the case of the 'heresy of the Indians', the Santidade de Jaguaripe in Bahia in the Northeast of Brazil in 1580.[27] In other places, the synthesis seems to have been virtually invisible. For example, a study of Christianity in early modern Japan claims that the so-called 'converts' incorporated Christian symbols into the indigenous symbolic system, producing a hybrid religion sometimes described as 'Kirishitan', from the Japanese way of pronouncing the word 'Christian'.[28]

The subject is immense but this essay is a short one. It offers a bird's-eye view of a terrain that is huge, varied and contested and makes an attempt to view the current debate on the globalization of culture in historical perspective.

Fernando Ortiz once described Cuban culture as a kind of stew, *ajiaco*.[29] A book about hybrid cultures can easily turn into a similar preparation, in which the ingredients, however various, are liquidized and homogenized. However, it is surely more illuminating to analyse mixture than to replicate it. In what follows I shall therefore try to draw distinctions rather than blurring them.

Hence the pages that follow will be divided into five

main chapters, united by their stress on variety. In the first place, the variety of *objects* that are hybridized. In the second place, the variety of *terms* and theories invented to discuss cultural interaction. Third, the variety of *situations* in which encounters take place. Fourth, the variety of possible *responses* to unfamiliar items of culture, and fifth and last, the variety of possible *outcomes* or consequences of hybridization over the long term.

ONE

Varieties of object

Examples of cultural hybridity are to be found everywhere, not only all over the globe but in most domains of culture – syncretic religions, eclectic philosophies, mixed languages and cuisines, and hybrid styles in architecture, literature or music. It would be unwise to assume that the term 'hybridity' has exactly the same meaning in all these cases. In order to grasp this eel, it may be useful to begin by distinguishing and discussing three kinds of hybridity, or processes of hybridization, respectively involving artefacts, practices and finally people. The discussion of alternative conceptualizations, such as 'cultural translation', will be postponed to chapter 2.

Hybrid artefacts

Architecture provides many instances of hybrid artefacts. For example, between the fourteenth and the seventeenth centuries, if not for longer, the city of L'viv (Lehmberg, Lwów, Lvov) in the western Ukraine was a multi-cultural city in which the different cultures interacted. When the Armenians constructed their cathedral in the fourteenth century, for instance, they commissioned an Italian architect, as did the Orthodox when they built a new church at the beginning of the seventeenth century. German, Italian and Armenian craftsmen all had their share in the creation of a local style of architecture that combined elements from their different traditions.[30]

Some examples of architectural hybridity still have the power to surprise if not to shock us, as in the case of churches or synagogues in Spain with fifteenth- or sixteenth-century geometrical decorations and even Arabic inscriptions (in the case of the church of San Roman in Toledo, for instance) recalling those of mosques, the work of craftsmen who were almost certainly Muslim or crypto-Muslim.[31] Conversely, in fifteenth-century India, mosques were sometimes built by Hindu craftsmen who made use of decorative formulae that they had learned in the process of constructing their own temples.[32]

Again, Jesuit missionaries from Goa to Cuzco employed local craftsmen to build their churches and colleges, and the results of the interaction between patrons and artisans were various combinations of Italian Renaissance or baroque structures with decorative details deriving from local traditions, whether these were Hindu, Islamic or Inca. In Peru, churches such as San Domingo in Cuzco were built on the site of Inca temples and even used stones from the original construction.[33]

On a smaller scale, furniture illustrates the same process of appropriation and adaptation. According to Gilberto Freyre, the straight lines and angles of English furniture were softened when the designs were copied in early nineteenth-century Brazil. North American furniture and pottery made by African-American craftsmen transformed English models in a similar way, suggesting that what Pierre Bourdieu called the 'habitus' of the artisans, the knowledge embodied in their hands and eyes, was African rather than European or American.[34] A more self-conscious case of hybridization is that of 'Chinese Chippendale', the name for a kind of eighteenth-century furniture that was inspired by China but made in England.

Images too can be hybrid, as the French historian Serge Gruzinski has shown in a remarkable study of the Christian art of Mexico in the first decades after the arrival of the missionaries. Most of the images were made by local craftsmen following European teachers (such as the Flemish lay brother Fray Pedro de Gante) or European models, such as paintings or engravings. Consciously or unconsciously, the local artists modified what they copied, assimilating it to their own traditions and producing what is sometimes known as 'Indo-Christian' art.[35]

A number of hyphenated phrases remind us that art

historians in particular have long been aware of the process of hybridization: among them are 'Hindu-Saracenic', 'Hispano-Mauresque' and 'Afro-Portuguese'.[36]

When Western images, especially engravings, arrived in China in the late sixteenth century together with Catholic missionaries such as Matteo Ricci, they helped transform the Chinese tradition of landscape painting. Chinese artists were not converted to the Western style – they resisted perspective, for instance – but awareness of an alternative to their own conventions for representing landscape liberated them from these conventions and allowed them to make innovations of their own.[37]

Two points with a much wider relevance emerge with particular clarity from discussions of hybrid images. In the first place, as art historians such as Aby Warburg (1866–1929) and Ernst Gombrich (1909–2001) as well as psychologists such as Richard Gregory (1923–) have all emphasized, stereotypes or schemata are necessary to the process of structuring perception and so interpreting the world. The eye depends on the brain. However, most if not all of these schemata come from the repertoires of particular cultures. Eye, brain and culture work together.[38]

In the second place, what we might call the 'affinities' or 'convergences' between images from different traditions affected the process of interaction. For example, the

Virgin Mary could be assimilated with apparent ease to other female goddesses such as Kuan Yin in China or Tonantzin in Mexico because she played an essentially similar role to these goddesses as a protective mother.[39]

Linguists sometimes speak of the 'convergence' between two languages that become increasingly similar as speakers of each borrow from the other. The point might be extended to cases where an initial similarity is amplified in the course of reproduction, as in the example of the German term for the sixteenth-century Swiss pikemen, moving between or combining *Landsknecht* (a young man from the countryside) and *lansquenet* (a man with a lance or pike).

Hybrid texts

Another important type of artefact is the text. Translations are the most obvious case of hybrid texts, since the search for what is often called 'equivalent effect' involves the introduction of words and ideas that are familiar to the new readers but might not be intelligible in the culture in which the book was originally written. The domestication of a foreign work is poised between plagiarism and imitation. A well-known case from the Renaissance is Nicolas Faret's *L'honnête homme* (1636), which may be regarded either as a plagiarization or as a free translation of Baldassare Castiglione's *Cortegiano* (1528).[40]

Literary genres too may be hybrids. The Japanese novel, the Arab novel, the African novel and possibly the Latin American novel as well should be regarded – and judged by critics – not as simple imitations of the Western novel but as literary hybrids, examples of 'narrative transculturation' as the Uruguyan critic Angel Rama (1926–83) called them, a combination of foreign techniques with local culture, especially popular culture.[41] These novels differ from the their Western models thanks not only to individual creativity but also to differences between the cultures in which they are produced and European cultural traditions.

There is little doubt, for instance, that the Brazilian writers Joaquim Machado de Assis (1839–1908) and José Lins do Rego (1901–57) owed a good deal to English predecessors, especially to Lawrence Sterne (1713–68) in the first case and Thomas Hardy (1840–1928) in the second. Reading Hardy inspired Lins to write regional novels, but these novels differ from their source of inspiration as much as the sugar plantations of Northeastern Brazil, about which Lins wrote, differed from the heaths and woods of Southwest England, described by Hardy. A similar point might be made about the relation between Yoknapatawpha County in the American South, as imagined by William Faulkner (1897–1962), and the Macondo of Gabriel García Márquez (1927–). García Márquez has declared his admiration for Faulkner but he has created his own world. As the English Jesuit poet Gerard Manley Hopkins (1844–89) wrote, 'The effect of studying masterpieces is to make me admire and do otherwise.'

The Egyptian writer Naguib Mahfouz (1911–2006) presents another example of cultural translation. He read many Western novels and confessed to a particular interest in Tolstoy, Dostoyevsky, Melville, Conrad, Lawrence, Thomas Mann and John Galsworthy.[42] His famous Cairo trilogy (1956–7) follows the fortunes of a single family over three generations between 1917 and 1944. In this respect the trilogy is reminiscent of Mann's *Buddenbrooks* and Galsworthy's *Forsyte Saga*, but, like the work of Lins and García Márquez, the novel is rooted in local soil.

Some non-Western novelists, in India and in Africa, for instance, have gone so far in the direction of the West as to write in English. All the same, their English interacts with their own mother tongues, producing what has been called a literary 'palimpsest', yet another metaphor for hybridity. Similar points might be made about Africans writing in French or in Portuguese. The language of many African 'novels', for instance, is distinctive. For example,

The Palm-Wine Drinkard (1952), by the Nigerian Amos Tutuola (1920–97), hovers between a written story and the oral performance of a folktale. It is written in what has been called an 'interlanguage', a form of English through which the writer's mother tongue, Yoruba, can often be heard. Tutuola has not only translated a folktale into English, he has translated English into semi-Yoruba.[43]

One of the leading African novelists of the twentieth century, another Nigerian, Chinua Achebe (1930–), has described his language as an English 'altered to suit its new African surroundings', taking words, phrases and proverbs from West African languages or from Anglo-African pidgin. Achebe situates himself at 'the cross-roads of cultures', that of the Igbo and that of the British.

The African novel is also situated at the cross-roads of genres, including not only the traditional oral folktale and the European novel, but also, in between the two, the popular texts written in English and produced in the 1960s in the market town of Onitsha in the Igbo-speaking part of Nigeria. Onitsha market literature, so called because the books were sold in the marketplace, was a twentieth-century African equivalent of traditional English 'chap-books', the French Bibliothèque Bleue or the Spanish *literatura de cordel*. It can hardly be coincidence that so many African novelists have come from the Onitsha region.[44]

20

Hybrid practices

Hybrid practices may be identified in religion, music, language, sport, festivals and other cultural domains. Mahatma Gandhi, for instance, has been described as creating 'his own religion, an idiosyncratic mixture of Hindu, Islamic, Buddhist and Christian, ideas'.[45] At a collective level, some relatively new religions offer particularly clear examples of hybridization.

Take, for example, the Brazilian cult Umbanda.[46] In Brazil, as in Haiti, Cuba and elsewhere, there have been centuries of interaction between West African gods and Catholic saints, still to be found in cults such as Candomblé in Brazil or Santería in Cuba, or the cult of the *orishas* in Trinidad – where the situation was made even more complicated in the twentieth century by interaction with Protestants (the 'Spiritual Baptists') and Hindus.

Ogun, for example, the god of iron and war and patron of the smiths, came to be identified with St George or St Michael; Shango, associated with thunder and lightning, with St John the Baptist or St Barbara; and Iemanjá, a mother goddess or sea goddess, with St Anne or with the Virgin Mary (sometimes known in Europe as 'the star of the sea', Stella Maris).[47]

In the case of Umbanda, to the mix of Candomblé and

Catholicism there was added the French cult known as *spiritisme* that was founded by Léon Hippolyte Rivail (1803–69) and emphasized contact with the spirits of the dead. Rivail's stress on spiritual evolution fitted the positivism of the period, while his references to *carma* are typical of late nineteenth-century Western interest in the wisdom of the East. Rivail believed in re-incarnation. Indeed, he adopted a new name, Allan Kardec, that of the druid he believed he had been in a former life.

In Brazil, 'Spiritism' or 'Kardecism', as it is often called, was an immediate success and the cult remains strong.[48] Umbanda arose from the encounter of Spiritism and Candomblé in Rio de Janeiro in the mid-1920s. In this case we find a deliberate syncretism rather than a gradual and semi-conscious interaction. The cult shares with Spiritism the concern with the spiritual purification of each individual, before and after death, but it shares with Candomblé the African gods who double as Catholic saints.

Again, take the variety of cultural traditions contributing to the Vietnamese religion Cao Dai, which was extremely successful in the years before the Communist regime was established over the whole country in the mid-1970s. Founded in 1926, Cao Dai has an organization modelled on the Catholic Church with a pope, cardinals and bishops. Its doctrines, on the other hand,

22

by Alejo Carpentier and Fernando Ortiz.[53] The *salsa* is still more of a mixture, since it originated in Cuba in the 1940s and was later influenced by jazz and by the music of Puerto Rico.

What the last example suggests – and many other examples as well – is that hybrid forms are often the result of multiple encounters rather than a single one. Sometimes new encounters reinforce old ones, as in the case of the Brazilian singer Gilberto Gil (1942–) who visited Senegal and Nigeria in the late 1970s in order to give his music a more African flavour. On other occasions, as in the case of *salsa*, successive meetings add new elements to the mix.

Yet another example of multiple hybridization is reggae, a form of music that originated in Jamaica in the 1970s and has since conquered much of the world, from Germany to Japan (where it is apparently perceived through cultural schemata derived from music associated with a local festival, O-Bon). The music includes British, African and North American elements. Reggae was introduced to Britain by Jamaican immigrants, who often lived in the same parts of London as other recent immigrants, including Indians. A Punjabi Englishman, Steve Kapur, who calls himself 'Apache Indian' and combines the tradition of reggae with that of Indian *bhangra* music, grew up in one of those parts of London.[54]

This is the moment to introduce an idea that will recur in these pages, the idea of cultural circularity. Some musicians in the Congo have been inspired by colleagues in Cuba, and some musicians in Lagos by colleagues in Brazil.[55] In other words Africa sometimes imitates Africa via America, making a circular tour, and yet one that does not end in the place that it started, since every imitation is also an adaptation.

Like music, language offers many striking examples of hybridization. The lyrics of reggae songs are written in a mixed language, Jamaican creole. In the case of Brazil, a vivid passage of Freyre's *The Masters and the Slaves* described how Portuguese became softer and smoother in the mouths of slaves, and how African nannies passed on this form of the language to the master's children.[56] The parallel with his point about Afro-Brazilian craftsmen smoothing out the angles of English furniture as they imitated it will be obvious enough.

In Europe too, examples of linguistic hybridization are not difficult to find. In the sixteenth and seventeenth centuries, for instance, the mixing of the European vernaculars with one another became more intense because contacts between languages were becoming more numerous. For one thing, migration within Europe was increasing. For another, the gradual decline of Latin and the increasing use of vernacular languages in print made it more necessary than before for Europeans to learn one another's languages.[57]

Yet another reason for linguistic hybridization at this time was the fact that European armies were growing, especially during the Thirty Years War (1618–48), and also becoming more international. The military speech community made a serious contribution to the mixing of languages because the mercenary armies of the period were international, polyglot, mobile organizations. Spanish, for example, provided technical terms such as *armada, camarada, emboscada, escalada* and *parada*, while French provided *avant-garde, bayonette, cadet, patrouille*, and Italian *battaglione, bombarda, infanteria, sentinello* and *squadrone*. Slightly modified, all these terms can be found in a wide range of European languages.[58]

Despite the rise of international rules for sport, it is not difficult to find examples of hybrid practices in this domain as well. A film made by an anthropologist in the Trobriand Islands (in Melanesia) is entitled *Trobriand Cricket*. The islanders learned the game from the English but they adapted it to allow hundreds of people to play on each side and also to carry spears, adapting a local form of ritualized warfare.[59]

Brazilian football offers a somewhat milder example of hybridization, following the formal international rules yet introducing a distinctive national style of play. As

Gilberto Freyre observed as long ago as 1938, 'The Brazilian mulatto de-europeanized football by giving it curves ... We dance with the ball.' An interview with a leading player of the 1930s, Domingos da Guia, confirmed this interpretation, since Domingos spoke of 'that short dribble I invented imitating the *miudinho*, that type of samba'.[60] Today, when cultural globalization carries football along with it and Brazilian players can be found in many European teams, this distinctively national style, or at any rate Latin style, may be in danger of disappearing as Europeans imitate the Brazilian style and Brazilians follow the instructions of European coaches.[61] If so, this will be yet another case of hybridization.

Hybridization is still more apparent in another of Brazil's leading cultural institutions: Carnival. Like other European institutions, the Carnival was transported to the New World, especially to that part of it which was colonized by Catholics from the Mediterranean. The so-called *entrudo*, in which people threw water or eggs at one another, was adopted with enthusiasm by both sexes and all social classes. The wearing of fancy dress and masks was another traditional European custom that was transported, and even some of the favourite costumes of the New World carnivals followed European models, from the hussars and harlequins of Rio de Janeiro to the

Pierrots and Punchinellos of Trinidad. The *desfile* of the Escolas de Samba in Rio today follows the tradition of the parades and the allegorical floats of fifteenth-century Florence and Nuremberg. Even the political references so common in Brazilian carnivals from the mid nineteenth century onwards have parallels in Europe – in seventeenth-century Spain, for example.[62]

However, like so many items of European culture, Carnival has been transformed in the course of its sojourn in the Americas. For example – as in the case of football – the importance of dancing makes New World carnivals distinctive, in Havana, Buenos Aires and Port of Spain no less than in Rio or Recife. The dance, whether religious or secular, was a particularly important art form in traditional Africa. Among the Yoruba of Dahomey and Nigeria, for example, ritualized dancing provoked the possession of the dancers by spirits or gods. In African religious rituals, women traditionally played an important part. It is probably these African traditions that explain the active role of women in the carnivals of the Americas, dancing in the street rather than simply observing from the balcony, as in Italy and elsewhere in Europe. In Brazil, female participation in the *entrudo* was already noted in the early nineteenth century by foreign visitors such as the Englishmen Henry Koster and John Mawe.[63]

We should avoid the temptation to see the Brazilian or the Cuban Carnival as a mixture of European and African ingredients that has set like a jelly in a mould. As in the case of many hybrid forms of culture, the mix is unstable. There have been waves of Europeanization, deliberate attempts by certain groups to 'whiten' the Carnival, as was the case in Rio in the mid nineteenth century, and waves of Africanization, especially in the last fifty years or so.[64] Again, the rise of Umbanda, described above, in the earlier twentieth century, was an attempt to whiten Candomblé, and was followed in the later twentieth century by an attempt to re-Africanize and purify it.[65]

Hybrid people

Hybrid people are crucial in all these processes. They include hybrid groups, like the Anglo-Irish, the Anglo-Indians and the African-Americans. The journal *Diasporas* (which began to appear in 1991) bears witness to increasing interest in the study of groups who for religious, political or economic reasons, have moved from one culture to another: Greeks from Constantinople after its capture by the Turks in 1453; Jews and Muslims from Andalusia after the fall of the Kingdom of Granada in

1492; Italians after 1870 to North America, South America and Australia; Chinese to South-East Asia or California in the nineteenth and twentieth centuries.

We must not forget hybrid individuals, whether they were born into this situation because their mothers and fathers came from different cultures, or entered it later, willingly or unwillingly, because they were, for example, converted or captured.[66] The theme of a life spent 'in between' different cultures recurs in recent autobiographies (Edward Said's, for instance, or Ien Ang's).[67] It can also be found in novels (such as the Chinese-American Maxine Hong Kingston's *Woman Warrior*), and in other forms of writing, including a book of mixed prose and poetry published by the Chicana writer Gloria Anzaldúa (1942–2004).[68] A life in between cultures often results in a 'double consciousness', to use the famous phrase of W. E. B. Du Bois (1868–1963) about North American blacks.[69]

Historians too have been exploring these themes.[70] The North American scholar Natalie Davis, for instance, has made a study of three seventeenth-century European women who lived on the margins or the cross-roads of cultures. The phenomenon of conversion, whether voluntary or forced, has also been attracting attention, as in the case of the so-called 'renegades' in the Ottoman Empire, Christians who turned Muslim.[71] A still more complex case, recently studied, is that of a 'man of three worlds', Samuel Pallache (died 1616), a Moroccan Jew who was active in both Catholic and Protestant Europe.[72]

Conversely, the sixteenth-century geographer known in the West as 'Leo the African' was converted from Islam to Christianity. Hasan al-Wazzân, to give him his Islamic name, was born in Granada. After the expulsion of the Muslims in 1492, his family moved to Fez, where he had a distinguished career as an envoy in the service of the local ruler. Captured by Sicilian pirates in 1518, Hasan was taken to Rome and presented to Pope Leo X. Converted to Christianity and baptized by the pope, Hasan took the name of Leo, and under this name wrote his famous description of Africa. He has been made the protagonist of a novel as well as the subject of a scholarly monograph. Appropriately enough, the authors of both books are themselves cultural hybrids, Arabs writing in French.[73]

Hasan al-Wazzân makes a good example of the hybrid as a cultural mediator. So do many translators, to be discussed later in this essay (pp. 100ff.), and a number of scholars, among them Ananda Coomaraswamy (1877–1947). Born in what was then the British colony of Ceylon to a Sinhalese father and an English mother, taken to England at the age of two but returning to Sri Lanka in his mid-twenties, Coomaraswamy made a career of mediating between the East and the West. He wrote books such as *Medieval Sinhalese Art* (1908), *The Indian Craftsman* (1909) and *Rajput Painting* (1916) and emphasized parallels between Asian art and that of the European Middle Ages as it had been viewed by Coomaraswamy's British gurus, John Ruskin (1819–1900), and William Morris (1834–96) whose famous press at Kelmscott in Gloucestershire he used to print his books.

TWO

Varieties of terminology

The variety of hybrid objects is more than matched by the number of terms that are current today in the writings of scholars describing the process of cultural interaction and its consequences. Indeed, far too many words are in circulation to describe the same phenomena. In the academic world, America has been rediscovered and the wheel has been re-invented again and again, essentially because scholars in one discipline have not been aware of what their neighbours were thinking. We live in a jungle of concepts competing for survival.

Many of the terms are metaphorical, making them at once more vivid and more misleading than plain language.[74] Five metaphors in particular dominate discussions, metaphors, drawn respectively, from economics, zoology, metallurgy, food and linguistics – borrowing, hybridity, the melting pot, the stew and, finally, translation and 'creolization'. As we have seen (above, p.1), the term 'hybridity' has been described as 'maddeningly elastic'. Unfortunately, this criticism applies to the rival terms as well.

The point of this chapter is not to claim that some of the terms in our intellectual toolbox are right and others are wrong. Nor is it to condemn the metaphors that proliferate in this domain, from 'hybridity' to 'creolization', even though I shall argue later that linguistic metaphors may well be more illuminating than their rivals. The main points to make are that all the terms, metaphorical and otherwise, need to be handled with care, and that it is easier to do this if we see the language that we use to analyse cultural mix, hybridity or translation as itself part of cultural history.

Cultural theory was not invented yesterday. On the contrary, it has gradually developed out of the way in which individuals and groups have reflected about cultural change over the centuries. It is surely axiomatic that scholars should take the views expressed by the people they are studying very seriously indeed. This axiom implies paying attention not only to 'local knowledge' as the American anthropologist Clifford Geertz has famously recommended, but also to what might be called 'local theory', to concepts such as 'imitation' or 'accommodation'.[75] In fact there are a number of important but unacknowledged similarities and continuities between the indigenous and the later theoretical concepts in this field, despite the obvious pejorative overtones of terms such as 'mongrel', 'bastard', 'mishmash' and so on.

Imitation and appropriation

In the history of the West, one of the ways in which cultural interaction has been discussed from classical antiquity onwards is via the idea of imitation. The positive side can be found in classical and Renaissance literary theory, in which creative imitation was presented as the emulation of Cicero, Virgil and other prestigious models.[75]

However, following a kind of double cultural standard, humanists who described themselves as engaged in creative imitation might still describe their colleagues as imitating in a slavish manner, as 'aping'. The same charge was levelled against people who followed foreign models in everyday life: Italian models in the Renaissance, French models in the seventeenth and eighteenth centuries, English models in the eighteenth and nineteenth centuries, and so on. Ironically enough, the critique of aping (*macaqueação*) by Padre Miguel do Sacramento Lopes Gama (1791–1852) and others in Brazil itself followed the very foreign models that the critics were condemning.[77]

An alternative to imitation was the idea of appropriation or, more vividly, 'despoiling' (*spolia*). The original context of the term was the discussion by theologians now revered as Fathers of the Church of the uses that early Christians were allowed to make of pagan culture.

Basil of Cesarea (*c.*329–79), for instance, argued for a selective appropriation of pagan antiquity, following the example of bees, who 'neither approach all flowers equally, nor try to carry away those they choose entire, but take only what is suitable for their work and leave the rest untouched'. This metaphor, which had already been used in a secular context by the Roman philosopher Seneca the younger (*c.*4 BC–AD 65) was to have a long career.[78]

Another Father of the Church, Augustine (354–430), quoting Exodus, used the more dramatic language of 'the spoils of the Egyptians'. Just as the Jews, when they left Egypt, took some Egyptian treasures with them, so Christians could legitimately re-employ items from classical culture, although it was pagan. Like zoology, the Bible was a treasury of metaphor. Augustine's predecessors Origen (*c.*185–*c.*254) and Jerome (*c.*347–420), quoting Deuteronomy, wrote about the classical tradition in similar terms as a beautiful captive, acceptable if her hair was shorn and her fingernails clipped.

The metaphor of the captive continued to be employed in the Middle Ages, by Thomas Aquinas (*c.*1225–74), for instance, and by Gregory IX (Pope, 1227–41).[79] Leaving aside what might now be described as the 'sexism' of the saints, and used to be called the misogyny of a celibate clergy, this aggressive language should be understood as the legitimation of an appropriation that could not be presented in a Christian context as imitation or borrowing.

This approach to cultural exchange was taken up once more at the Renaissance and it has been revived once again in our own time. Whether consciously or unconsciously, contemporary theorists of appropriation, notably the French Catholics Michel de Certeau (1925–86) and Paul Ricoeur (1913–2005), have drawn on the Christian tradition. One might describe this process as 'the spoils of Augustine', the re-employment of the idea of re-employment.[80] Indeed, in his *L'Invention du quotidien* (1980), in which the idea of *ré-emploi* was expounded, Certeau referred directly to this passage from Augustine, writing of readers 'ravissant les biens d'Égypte pour en jouir'. He did not cite Augustine by name, as if the point was too familiar to require elucidation.[81]

The famous discussions of 'anthropophagy' in early twentieth-century Brazil are a variant of this approach, concerned as they were with taking something alien and digesting it. The metaphor of digestion is an old one, used by Seneca, among others, in the ancient world and revived at the Renaissance, as in the epigram of Francis Bacon (1561–1626) in his essay 'Of Studies': 'Some books are to be tasted, others to be swallowed, and some few to be chewed and digested.' However, it is in South

America and especially in Brazil that the metaphor has been most used and elaborated.

In 1924, for instance, the Argentinian poet Oliverio Girondo (1891–1967) wrote about 'our capacity to digest and assimilate' ('nuestra capacidad digestiva y de asimilación').[82] Most famously, in his *Manifesto antropófago* (1928) the Brazilian writer Oswald de Andrade (1890–1954) addressed the question whether or not to follow European models by playing with the idea of cannibalism. He attacked the 'importers of canned consciousness', claiming that Brazilians were capable of digesting foreign ideas, thus making them their own. Again, in the 1950s, he described the Brazilians as 'champions of miscegenation, both racially and culturally'. More recently, the singer-composer Caetano Veloso (1942–) took up the metaphor to defend himself and his colleagues against the charge of following foreign models, declaring that 'we are eating the Beatles and Jimi Hendrix'.[83]

The negative side of the idea of appropriation can be found in accusations of plagiarism, which began long before the laws of copyright came into force. In classical Latin, the term *plagiarius* originally referred to someone who kidnapped a slave, but it was applied by the poet Martial to literary theft. The term was revived at the Renaissance, when it became commonplace for writers to accuse one another of robbery ('larceny' in English, *larcin* in French, *ladroneccio* in Italian and so on).

A milder term of the same class is that of cultural 'borrowing'. It was often a pejorative term, as in the case of the French scholar-printer Henri Estienne (*c.*1528–98), for instance, a linguistic purist who wrote of 'incompetent householders' ('mauvais ménagers'), borrowing from their neighbours what they already have at home. In similar fashion, Adamantios Korais (1748–1833), one of the leaders of the movement for Greek independence, denounced 'borrowing from strangers ... words and phrases amply available in one's own language'. In nineteenth-century Russia, there was a major debate from the 1840s onwards about the value and the dangers of borrowing from Western Europe. There was a similar debate in South America. The Brazilian writer Euclides da Cunha (1866–1909), for example, denounced his own culture as 'a culture of borrowing' ('uma cultura de empréstimo').[84]

It is surely significant that the term 'borrowing' acquired a more positive sense in the second half of the twentieth century. According to the French historian Fernand Braudel (1902–85), for instance, it was necessary for a living culture to be able both to give and to receive, to lend and to borrow ('pour une civilisation, vivre c'est à la fois être capable de donner, de recevoir, d'emprunter'). Edward Said declared that 'The history of all cultures is the history of cultural borrowing.'[85] For linguists, 'borrowing' has long been a neutral, descriptive term.[86] In similar fashion, Paul Ricoeur and other cultural theorists use the term 'appropriation' without disapproval.

A more technical term is 'acculturation', coined around 1880 by anthropologists in the USA who were working on the cultures of the Native Americans.[87] The essential idea was that of a subordinate culture adopting traits from the dominant culture. In other words, 'assimilation', a word frequently used in discussions that took place in the early twentieth century about the culture of the new wave of immigrants to the United States. The Cuban sociologist Fernando Ortiz came closer to the contemporary idea of reciprocity when he suggested replacing the notion of one-way 'acculturation' by two-way 'transculturation'. As he remarked, we should not think in simple terms of Columbus discovering America, since the Americans in their turn discovered Columbus.[88]

Another technical term is that of 'transfer', coined by economic historians and historians of technology but now used more widely to refer to other kinds of borrowing.[89] A recent example of this wider usage comes from a project of collective research financed by the European Science Foundation and directed by the French historian Robert Muchembled under the bilingual title 'Cultural Exchange / Transferts culturels'.[90]

41

The phrase 'cultural exchange' has also come into general use only recently, although it was already employed in the work of the German scholar Aby Warburg early in the twentieth century.[91] Its popularity today, replacing older terms like 'borrowing', owes something to an increasing relativism of the kind expressed by Ortiz. However, the term 'exchange' should not be taken to imply that any cultural movement in one direction is associated with an equal but opposite movement in the other: the relative importance of the two directions is a matter for empirical research.

Accommodation and negotiation

A traditional concept that has been enjoying a revival is that of 'accommodation'. In ancient Rome, Cicero used this term in a rhetorical context, to refer to the need for orators to adapt their style to their audience. Early medieval Europeans, notably Pope Gregory the Great, adapted the concept to a religious context, noting the need to make the Christian message acceptable to the the pagans in England and elsewhere. According to Gregory, pagan temples should not be destroyed but converted into churches, in order to facilitate the acceptance of the new religion. In a later age of Christian missions, the sixteenth and seventeenth centuries, the building of churches on the site of temples, as in the case of San Domingo (above, p. 14), followed Gregory's recommendations.

Following this model, sixteenth-century missionaries like the Italian Jesuit Matteo Ricci (1552–1610) spoke of the 'accommodation' of Christianity to new environments such as China. In this way, Ricci justified his practice of dressing as a Confucian scholar in order to bring the religious ideas he was preaching closer to the Chinese, and also of allowing converts to carry on the traditional practice of ancestor worship, which Ricci decided to interpret as a social custom, not a form of religion. Ricci translated the word 'God' by the neologism 'Tianzhu', literally 'Lord of Heaven', and allowed Chinese Christians to refer simply to 'Tian', 'Heaven', in the manner of Confucius.[92]

In Japan, too, some Jesuits followed the method of accommodation, wearing silk robes, eating in the Japanese manner and calling God by one of the names of Buddha, 'Dainichi'.[93] In similar fashion to Ricci, his fellow-Italian and fellow-Jesuit Roberto de' Nobili (1577–1656) – who worked in South India, dressed as a local holy man and allowed his Brahmin converts to retain their sacred threads – defended himself against the charge of tolerating paganism by quoting Gregory the Great.[94]

Recently, the term 'accommodation' has been revived, notably by historians of religion who are critical of the concepts of 'acculturation' (because it implies a complete change) and 'syncretism' (because it suggests a deliberate mixture). However, the term is changing its meaning to include both partners in the encounter, the 'converted' as well as the missionaries. As scholars try harder than before to see religious encounters from both sides, they are becoming increasingly convinced that the result was not so much conversion as some form of hybridization.

Thus a recent account of the Jesuits in China argues that the mandarins practised accommodation no less than the Jesuits.[95] They did not see themselves – as the Jesuits saw them – as replacing Confucianism with Christianity. On the contrary, they regarded the new belief system as complementary to the traditional one. Cultural change took place, as it so often does, by addition rather than by substitution.

Alternative terms to 'accommodation' in recent studies are 'dialogue' and 'negotiation', both of them emphasizing the view from below as well as the view from above, and the initiatives taken by the converted as well as those of the missionaries.[96]

The concept of negotiation in particular has become increasingly popular in cultural studies in a number of contexts. At a micro-level it has been used to analyse both plea bargaining in courts and discussions of illness between patients and doctors, conversations that lead both parties to revise their original diagnoses. At a macro-level, the term has been employed to analyse the dialogue between two intellectual systems – elite and popular, for example – or the system of the missionaries and that of the people they are trying to convert.[97] The term is frequently employed in analyses of ethnicity because it expresses an awareness of the multiplicity and fluidity of identity and the way in which it can be modified or at least presented in different ways in different situations.[98] Translation too is sometimes presented as a process of negotiating meanings.[99]

Mixing, syncretism, hybridity

In the sixteenth and seventeenth centuries, the process of accommodation was sometimes criticized as leading to mixing or syncretism. Mixture, 'hotchpotch' or 'mish-mash' was viewed as a kind of disorder. In sixteenth-century Mexico, the Dominican friar Durán used pejorative and sometimes culinary terms such as 'mezclar' and even 'salad' when he referred to the religion of the people.[100]

Like the mixing of religious beliefs, the mixing of languages was often criticized at this time, again in culinary terms such as 'kitchen Latin' or 'macaronic' Latin. English and Yiddish were both condemned as corrupt or mixed languages. On the other hand, Martin Luther, anticipating modern linguists, once remarked that 'All languages are mixed' ('Omnes linguae inter se permixtae sunt').[101] Today, the concept of a 'mixed language' has become respectable in linguistics, and both the *media lengua* of Ecuador and the 'mix-mix' of the Philippines are now the objects of serious study.[102]

Brazilian historians might consider paying similar attention to the Italo-Portuguese spoken in São Paulo in the early twentieth century, drawing on the letters of recent immigrants as well as on the stylized 'macaronic' language of comic literary figures such as Juó Bananére.[103] In this case, it is particularly clear that hybridity is often, if not always, a process rather than a state, since this macaronic language marked a particular stage in the assimilation of the immigrants into Brazilian culture.

A metallic metaphor with a similar function is that of 'fusion'. Thus the German botanist and explorer Karl von Martius (1794–1868) suggested that the history of Brazil might be written in terms of the 'fusion' of three races, while Gilberto Freyre wrote of 'the harmonious fusion of diverse traditions'. In Mexico, Manuel Gamio (1883–1960), a pupil of the German-American anthropologist

Franz Boas (1858–1942) and the author of a book enti-tled *Forging the Fatherland* (1916) – organized around the extended metallic metaphor of the blacksmith, the anvil, the forge, iron and bronze – supported what he called 'the fusion of races' or 'fusion of cultural manifestations'.

Today, the language of fusion, perhaps inspired by nuclear physics, has become popular in contexts ranging from music to cuisine. 'Asian fusion', for instance, refers to restaurants that serve a variety of oriental cuisines. Musicologists now speak about 'fusion genres'. 'Jazz fusion', for instance, refers to a musical style that mixes or fuses jazz with funk, rock, classical, folk and other musics.

The idea of fusion is not far from the famous metaphor of the United States as a cultural 'melting pot'. The passing of this term into ordinary language was encouraged by its choice as the title of a once-controver-sial play by the Jewish writer Israel Zangwill (1864–1926), who was born in London into a family that had recently arrived from Russia. *The Melting Pot* opened in New York in 1908 and dramatized the acceptance of immigrants as 'Americans' in 'God's Crucible, the great Melting Pot where all the races of Europe are melting and refining'. A similar metallic term, less successful, is 'amal-gamation', used on occasion by Melville Herskovits.[104]

As for 'syncretism', a word first used by the Greek

writer Plutarch (*c.*46–120) in the sense of a political alliance, it came to be re-employed in the seventeenth century to deplore efforts like those of the Lutheran theologian Georg Calixtus (1586–1656) to unite different groups of Protestants. It meant a kind of religious chaos. Positive terms for similar processes included 'consensus' (used by Calixtus about his own goal) and 'conciliatio', employed to describe the efforts of some Renaissance scholars, such as Giovanni Pico della Mirandola (1463–94), to reconcile Christianity with paganism.[105]

In the late nineteenth century, the word 'syncretism' acquired a positive meaning in the context of studies of religion in classical antiquity carried out by the Belgian scholar Franz Cumont (1868–1947) and others.[106] It is used in particular to discuss the identifications, so common in the Hellenistic period, between gods or goddesses from different cultures (the Phoenician goddess Astarte, for example, was identified with Aphrodite, and the Egyptian god of writing, Thoth, with Hermes).[107]

From the classics, the term passed into other disciplines. The American anthropologist Melville Herskovits, for example, found that the concept of syncretism 'helped to sharpen' his analyses of culture contact, especially in the case of African-American religion (as in the case of the identification between St Barbara and the god

Shango, mentioned above). On the other hand, it attracted criticism from those who complained that Herskovits ignored the people involved, the social actors.[108]

The more vivid botanical or biological metaphor of 'hybridity' or *mestizaje* was especially popular in the nineteenth and twentieth centuries, emerging from traditional terms of abuse such as 'mongrel' or 'bastard' and producing synonyms such as 'cross-fertilization'.[109]

In the work of Gilberto Freyre, for instance, this idea was a central one, described in his rich vocabulary in a variety of different ways. The concepts of *métissage* and *interpénétration* were also central in the analyses of African-American religion by the French sociologist Roger Bastide (1898–1974), an admirer, if not exactly a disciple, of both Herskovits and Freyre.[110]

It was and is in the Spanish and the Spanish-American world, however, that the idea of *mestizaje* has been employed most frequently, in both the literal sense of interbreeding and the metaphorical sense of the 'intermingling of cultures'. Sometimes it has been a term of abuse, sometimes a term of praise, and on other occasions an instrument of academic analysis. The Basque anthropologist Telesforo Aranzadi Unamuno (1860–1945), a cousin of the philosopher Miguel Unamuno, defended cultural mixing. The writer Ramiro de Maeztu y

Whitney (1875–1936), himself of mixed origin (his mother was English), defined *hispanidad* as a mixture, and so did the historian Américo Castro, discussed above.

In Mexico, Vicente Riva Palacio (1832–96), a Darwinian who believed that interbreeding would lead to something new, argued that the *mestizo* was the race of the future, an idea now associated with José Vasconcelos. In Argentina, the writers Leopoldo Lugones (1874–1938) and Ricardo Rojas (1882–1957) both made *mestizaje* central to their definitions of the national identity.[111]

In a very different location, both geographical and intellectual, the Russian literary theorist Mikhail Bakhtin (1895–1975) also drew attention to the importance of the cultural hybrid and of hybridization (*gibrid, gibridizacija*). For example, he described the sixteenth-century satire *The Letters of Obscure Men* as 'a complex intentional linguistic hybrid' of Latin and German, illustrating what he called the 'inter-illumination' ('vznaimnoosveščenie') of languages. According to Bakhtin, his inter-illumination reached its highest point during the Renaissance and helped stimulate literary innovation and creativity, most obviously in the works of François Rabelais, to whom he devoted a whole book. The idea of the hybrid was linked to two concepts that were central to Bakhtin's thought, 'heteroglossia' (*raznorečie*) and 'polyphony' (*polifoniya*). 'Heteroglossia' refers to the diversity of language within a single text, and 'polyphony' to the different voices adopted by novelists such as Dostoyevsky.[112]

Today, the term 'hybridity' is a recurrent one in post-colonial studies – in the work of Edward Said, for instance. 'All cultures are involved in one another', wrote Said of our present situation, 'none is single and pure, all are hybrid, heterogeneous'.[113] Although he treats the term with more ambivalence (or rather, stresses its ambivalence), the idea of hybridity is also central to the work of Homi Bhabha.[114]

Much less well known today but equally illuminating, so it may be argued, in the analysis of cultural change, is the concept of the oicotype employed by the Swedish folklorist Carl Wilhelm von Sydow (1878–1952). Like 'hybridity', the word 'oicotype' or 'ecotype' was originally coined by botanists to refer to a variety of plant adapted to a certain milieu by natural selection. Von Sydow borrowed the term in order to analyse changes in folktales, which he viewed as adapted to their cultural milieu.[115] Scholars who study cultural interactions might appropriately follow Sydow's paradigm and discuss local forms – Czech baroque architecture, for example – as regional variants of an international movement, variants that have their own rules.

51

In the history of ideas, as has been noted already, the wheel is often rediscovered: that is, scholars working on one problem or in one discipline often discover a phenomenon that scholars working on another problem in another discipline have known for a long time. In the debate on globalization that is currently taking place, a recurrent question concerns the extent of cultural homogenization, sometimes discussed in terms of 'Coca-colonization' or 'McDonaldization'. Some scholars stress the importance of a countermovement of heterogenization, citing examples of the adaptation of global products – including Coca-Cola and McDonald's – to local situations.

In the case of Coca-Cola, for instance, local brands, such as Inka Kola in Peru, have sprung up in competition with the North American ones. In Trinidad and elsewhere, Coke is often mixed with local drinks such as rum or brandy. It may serve new functions – in China, for instance, it is heated and drunk as medicine. A newspaper report about Indians in Mexico claimed that they had incorporated Pepsi into their religious rituals.[116]

As for McDonald's, the standardization of the hamburger is a key to the international success of the enterprise. Indeed, some economists measure the performance of different economies by comparing the prices for a Big Mac. However, this standardization has come to coexist with adaptations of the product to the needs of certain national markets. The company sells McHuevo in Uruguay, McBurrito in Mexico, and the Maharaja Mac in India (replacing beef with lamb). Reactions to the spread of the chain of restaurants in Japan, Korea, China and Taiwan have been studied by a team of five American anthropologists. The restaurants were generally considered to be expensive, so that visiting them was a sign of a special occasion, which might justify taking a taxi. So what was their appeal? They offered an example and a sign of Western modernity, thanks not only to the hygienic surroundings but also to the self-service and the queues, symbols of democracy. In a sense, what the customers were buying was a slice of the American way of life.[117]

Examples such as these have encouraged analysts of globalization to use the term 'localization', borrowed from the software industry, or the word 'glocalization', originally business jargon of the 1980s.[118] Folklorists who follow this debate must have a sense of *déjà vu*, since we are witnessing what might be called the return of the oicotype.

The existence of oicotypes is a reminder that we need to be aware of centrifugal forces as well as centripetal ones. Like the history of languages and dialects, the history of culture in general may be viewed as a struggle between these two forces. Sometimes one tendency is in the ascendant, sometimes the other, but they achieve a kind of balance over the long term.

Concepts in question

Concepts are supposed to help us to solve intellectual problems, but they not infrequently create problems themselves. More exactly, each concept encourages its users to become aware of problems that alternative concepts obscure. In the case of 'appropriation', for example, we surely need to ask who appropriates what and for what purposes. In other words, it is necessary to discover the logic of choice, the rationale, conscious or unconscious, for selecting some items from a repertoire while rejecting others. The concept of syncretism encourages us to investigate the extent to which the different elements are blended (as anyone who has used a kitchen blender knows, there are degrees of fusion).[119] As for 'hybridity', it is a slippery, ambiguous term, at once literal and metaphorical, descriptive and explanatory.[120]

The concepts of mixing and hybridity also suffer from the disadvantage of appearing to exclude individual agency. 'Mixing' sounds too mechanical. 'Hybridity' evokes the outside observer studying culture as if it were nature, and the products of individuals and groups as if they were botanical specimens. Concepts such as 'appropriation' and 'accommodation' throw more light on human agency and creativity. So does the increasingly widespread idea of 'cultural translation', a phrase employed to describe the mechanism by which cultural encounters produce new and hybrid forms.

Cultural translation

Of the different metaphors used to describe the subject of this essay, it is the linguistic one that appears, to me at least, to be the most helpful and the least misleading. One form that it takes is the phrase 'cultural translation', first used by anthropologists. Bronisław Malinowski (1884–1942), for example, a Pole who migrated to England and carried out fieldwork in Melanesia, claimed that 'the learning of a foreign culture is like the learning of a foreign tongue' and that, through his books, he was attempting 'to translate Melanesian conditions into our own'. However, the idea that understanding an alien culture was analogous to the work of translation first became current among anthropologists in the 1950s and 1960s.

A key figure in this transition is the British anthropologist Edward Evans-Pritchard (1902–73), who was writing in 1951 about 'translation from one culture to another' and the skill necessary 'to translate a foreign culture into the language of one's own'.[121] His followers, such as Godfrey Lienhardt and Thomas Beidelman, continued his use of the concept and one went so far as to declare that 'Anthropology is an art of translation.'[122]

The original context for the rise of the metaphor was the practical problem of how to render key terms used by the peoples being studied when they had no equivalents in the languages spoken by the anthropologists. Since historians face a similar problem, it was only to be expected that some of them would be attracted by the idea.[123]

However, the use of the metaphor 'translation of culture' is no longer confined to philosophical or semi-philosophical discussions of what anthropologists or cultural historians do. It has been extended to include the thoughts and actions of everyone. The crucial insight underlying this extension occurred to the German Romantics and has been expressed with exemplary brevity by the cosmopolitan literary critic George Steiner: 'When we read or hear any language-statement from the past ... we translate'. Or again: 'inside or between languages, human communication equals translation'.[124]

A cultural historian might want to add the suggestion that the metaphor describes some human situations better than others, especially situations in which people from one culture encounter people from another. For example, when Vasco da Gama and his men entered a temple in Calicut, on the southwest coast of India, in 1498, they were confronted with an unfamiliar image, the conjoined heads of Brahma, Vishnu and Shiva, the three main gods of the Hindus. The Portuguese visitors perceived this image as a representation of the Holy Trinity. In other words, they 'translated' it into familiar terms by drawing on the visual schemata or stereotypes current in their own culture. In this case, the act of translation was probably unconscious.

Again, we may describe missionaries such as Matteo Ricci, concerned with religious 'accommodation', as attempting to translate Christianity – consciously, this time – from one cultural system to another. In similar fashion, the phrase 'the translation of gods', coined by the German Egyptologist Jan Assmann, is an illuminating way of describing what used to be known as 'syncretism', in other words the search for equivalents in the pantheon of one culture for major figures in the pantheon of another.[125]

In the ancient world, for instance, as we have seen, the Egyptian god of writing, Thoth, was equated with or translated into the Greek Hermes and the Roman Mercury, while the Phoenician goddess Astarte was translated into the Greek Aphrodite and the Roman Venus. In similar fashion, many centuries later, the encounter between traditional African cults and European Catholicism in the New World generated a whole series of equivalents or translations, some of which have already been mentioned, such as Shango – St Barbara and Ogun – St George.[126]

In the history of art or music, it may be illuminating to think in similar terms. For example, a recent study of the *alla turca* style of music, a Western style inspired by the music of the Ottoman Empire, has described it as 'a set of principles of translation as much as (or more than) a set of imitative devices'.[127] This insight is probably applicable to other genres and illustrates with particular clarity the value of the term as a more subtle alternative to simple ideas of imitation.

The term 'translation' has two advantages. In the first place, the advantage of emphasizing the work that needs to be done by individuals and groups to domesticate the alien, and the strategies and the tactics that they employ. In the second place, the advantage of neutrality, with associations of cultural relativism. This was indeed one of the reasons for its original appeal to anthropologists. 'Translation' contrasts with value-laden terms such as 'misunderstanding', 'misinterpretation', 'misrecognition', 'misreading', 'mistranslation' or 'misuse'.[128]

This contrast between neutral and value-laden terminology raises the question whether it is possible to make cultural mistranslations. What makes the question difficult to answer is the lack of agreed criteria for what would constitute such a mistranslation. All the same, it is tempting to use this phrase to describe Matteo Ricci's decision to dress as a Buddhist monk when he first arrived in China. He made the decision because he saw Buddhist monks as the local equivalent of Catholic priests, but he abandoned it when he learned that these monks had a low status in the eyes of the Confucian elite who were the main target of his missionary activities. In other words, Ricci himself recognized that he had made a mistake and proceeded to rectify it by dressing as a scholar.

However, in cases where individuals and groups persist in their cultural translations, it is surely unwise for posterity to take sides. What we surely need to do is to take account of the opposite points of view of the donors – that is, individuals from the culture from which a particular item has been appropriated – and of the receivers. For donors, any adaptation or translation of their culture looks like an error. On the other hand, receivers may equally well perceive their own adjustments as the correction of mistakes. In a delightful and illuminating evocation of her fieldwork, the American anthropologist Laura Bohannan once described how she told the story of *Hamlet* to a group of West Africans. The older men insisted on correcting her 'mistakes' and explaining to her the 'true meaning' of the story, adapting it to their culture as they did so.[129]

One problem that these disagreements reveal with clarity is the problem of translatability. Although many attempts at cultural translation have been made, it does not follow that items of culture are fully translatable. This point is perhaps most obvious in the case of language. Speakers of a number of languages often claim that a particular term is untranslatable, that something important is lost in the search for equivalents, as in the case of the German *Bildung* (more or less 'education'), the Russian *byt* (more or less 'way of life') or the Portuguese *saudade* (more or less 'nostalgia').

Indeed, thinking about the possible direction of future research in cultural studies, it might be fruitful if scholars were to pay more attention to what in a given culture most resists translation, and to what is lost in the process of translation from one culture to another.

Something may also be lost when we view cultural exchanges in terms of translation. 'Cultural translation' is a metaphor which, like other metaphors, is both illuminating and misleading. It forms part of a package of metaphors, associated as it is with the idea of cultures as texts that may be read by anthropologists, archaeologists or historians. If we are tempted by this metaphor, we need to stop and ask ourselves in what ways a culture differs from a text. The linguistic metaphor may be less dangerous than the botanical metaphor of 'hybridity', but it retains the capacity to lead unwary users astray.

Creolization

Other linguistic models have been extended to different forms of culture. For example, one critic of the term 'hybridity' has suggested that we replace it by the phrase 'cultural diglossia', adapting the model of two languages or two varieties of language used by the same people in different situations, often distinguishing a 'higher' language or variety from a 'lower' one.[130]

More widespread today is the use of the cultural model of 'creolization'. The term 'creole' has been employed for centuries in Spanish, Portuguese, French and English to describe people born in the Americas (or on islands such as Madagascar or Réunion) whose ancestors came from other continents (mainly Europe but sometimes the continent of Africa). Generalizing from studies of the Caribbean, linguists have come to employ the term 'creolization' to describe the situation in which a former *lingua franca* or pidgin develops a more complex structure, as people begin to use it for general purposes or even to learn it as their first language.[131] Building on their affinities or congruences, two languages in contact change to become more like each other and so 'converge' to create a third, which often takes most of its vocabulary from one of the parent languages and its structure or syntax from the other. In the case of the *media lengua* of Ecuador, for instance, the vocabulary is mainly Spanish while the structure comes from Quechua.[132]

Following this model but also broadening it, some scholars have written about the 'creolization' of whole cultures, not only in the Americas but elsewhere as well. Some scholars have argued that the term should be restricted to the Americas, where it originated, or even to the Caribbean.[133] Without denying the specificity of the cultures of the Caribbean, however, it might be argued that the uprooting experienced by slaves coming to the Americas revealed certain cultural processes with particular clarity, so that the concept of creolization does have useful work to do in several continents as well as in several disciplines.

The Swedish anthropologist Ulf Hannerz has described creole cultures as those that have had time 'to move towards a degree of coherence' and 'can put things together in new ways', creating a 'new culture' out of the 'confluence' of 'two or more cultural currents'.[134] A number of Anglophone scholars have suggested the relevance of this linguistic model for the study of the development of African-American religion, music, housing, clothing and cuisine. They have studied the process of cultural convergence in particular places and periods, such as Jamaica in the seventeenth century, once again using the term 'creolization' to refer to the emergence of new cultural forms out of the mixture of old ones.[135]

A similar point might be made about Brazil, where different African cultures merged and mixed with indigenous and Portuguese traditions to produce a new order, or about Spanish America, where, independently of the Anglophone world, historians such as the Argentinian José Luis Romero (1909–77) used the term 'acriollarse' to refer to the way in which the descendants of the Spanish settlers adopted indigenous products and indigenous customs in the colonial period. Indeed, he devoted a chapter of his book on Latin American cities to 'creole cities'.[136]

The concept of creolization has begun to be used still more broadly to discuss European cultures, for instance, or intellectual disciplines. Even the history of science has begun to be discussed in these terms, in a work that describes people from the different 'sub-cultures' of twentieth-century physics (experimenters, for example, and theorists) communicating in a mixed language that might be described as a scientific pidgin or creole.[137]

In these studies, language functions not as a metaphor

63

but as a model, employed self-consciously and systematically and making particular use of the distinction between vocabulary and grammar or deep structure. The idea of 'convergence' is turning out to be useful outside as well as inside the linguistic domain in which it was originally formulated.[138] Herskovits, for instance, wrote of the 'convergence' between African gods and Catholic saints in the New World, emphasizing the idea of process that is present but less obvious in concepts such as 'mixing' or 'syncretism. Describing the same situation, Bastide wrote of 'rapprochements'.[139]

The success of the idea of cultural translation may be linked to the linguistic turn and especially to the idea of culture as a text: a metaphor long favoured by anthropologists, from Claude Lévi-Strauss (1908–) to Clifford Geertz (1926–2006), but not theirs alone. Borrowing concepts from the Danish linguist Louis Hjelmslev (1899–1965), the French structuralist critic Roland Barthes (1915–80) analysed the language of clothes. The Russian semiotician Juri Lotman (1922–93) constructed what he called a 'poetics' of everyday life. Paul Ricoeur wrote about 'meaningful action considered as a text'.[140] The metaphor is illuminating but also dangerous. We surely need to think not only about analogies but also about dis-analogies, looking for the ways in which a culture differs from a text. We should ask ourselves what is lost in cultural translation, what is obscured when we employ this particular concept.

To sum up this chapter: although there are still too many terms and concepts in circulation to describe and analyse the processes that are the subject of this volume, we do need a number of them to do justice both to human agency (as in the case of 'appropriation' or 'cultural translation') and to changes of which the agents are unaware (as in the case of 'hybridization' or 'creolization'). An awareness of alternative concepts offers a defence against the confusion of concepts with the world they are used to analyse.

THREE

Varieties of situation

Another reason for retaining a variety of concepts is that the differences of situation, context and locale in which cultural encounters occur require an appropriate vocabulary for their analysis. It is surely true, as the epigraphs to this book suggest, that every culture is hybrid and that the process of hybridization takes place all the time. All the same, some cultures are surely more hybrid than others. There are also moments of particularly intense hybridization, the consequence of cultural encounters.

Following these moments, a kind of stabilization takes place, so that when there is another encounter and another wave of hybridization, the traditional hybrid culture is defended against the new mix. Well-known examples of this phenomenon could be found in South America, especially in Argentina and Brazil, in the late nineteenth century. At this point a new wave of Italian migrants threatened to upset the old cultural equilibrium: in Argentina between Spaniards and Amerindians, in Brazil between Portuguese, Amerindians and Africans.

Besides a geography and a chronology of hybridization, there is also a sociology, little explored so far. When cultures meet, some individuals and groups participate in the process more than others. In the case of the British in India, for instance, it has been argued that 'British conquest and rule mobilized latent, deviant or minority qualities within traditional Indian society' that were similar to, or compatible with, British values.[141] This example of what is called 'convergence' elsewhere in this volume helps to explain why different cultural encounters have led to more or less intense hybridization.

Besides distinguishing between moments and social groups, we may also distinguish between encounters of equals and unequals, between traditions of appropriation and resistance, and between locales of encounter, from the metropolis to the frontier.

Equals and unequals

The stories of cultural encounters between equals in power and those between unequals have very different plots. There was, for example, a striking contrast between the techniques of Catholic missionaries in China (Matteo Ricci, for instance) and their colleagues in Mexico, Peru or Brazil. In China, the missionaries were in a tiny minority. The situation therefore favoured the cultural 'borrowers' rather than the 'lenders'. The European missionaries were forced to persuade their listeners, in other words to adapt themselves to the indigenous culture, to meet it halfway. Following their motto (borrowed by Ignatius Loyola from St Paul) of being 'all things to all people', the Jesuits accommodated themselves to the local culture so effectively that they were accused by their critics of having been converted by the Chinese.[142]

The missionaries in Mexico and Peru, on the other hand, were able to use force or the threat of force to impose Christianity on the Indians. Cultural exchange in colonial Spanish and Portuguese America did not take place on equal terms. The initiative was usually with the lender, even if it is possible to perceive examples of what has been described as 'reverse acculturation' in some domains, as the colonizers gradually adopted indigenous items of culture, ranging from tobacco to the hammock.[143]

In the case of the interaction between Christianity and African religions, two very different kinds of situation need to be distinguished. One is that of the acceptance of Christianity by African rulers. The missionaries believed that they had achieved conversions, but there is evidence that the rulers saw themselves as simply incorporating new and powerful practices into their traditional religion. It is also possible that the two sides were at least partly aware of their differences but chose not to speak or even think about them, thus creating what has been called a 'working misunderstanding' that avoided open conflict.[144]

This situation may be contrasted with that of the African slaves in the Americas, who sometimes conformed outwardly to Christianity, especially in the first generations of slavery, while retaining their traditional beliefs. The 'translation' of Ogun, Shango or Iemanjá into their Catholic equivalents may have been originally a kind of camouflage, allowing African cults to survive among the slaves in the New World. However, what probably began as a conscious defence mechanism gradually developed over the centuries into something else.

Take, for instance, the cult known in some parts of Brazil as Candomblé. Originally a Yoruba cult from West Africa, it has been modified, consciously or unconsciously, in its new environment. Priests have become less important, for instance, and each individual had his or her own *orixá* or god (a term often translated in Brazil as *santo*, revealing the interpenetration of African cults with Catholicism). In any case, 'nearly all Candomblé adherents consider themselves to be good Catholics'.[145] One cult leader told a visiting anthropologist that 'I was baptized Catholic like every Brazilian. But I also serve the *orixás*. And anyway, there's only one God.'[146]

Placing the emphasis on equivalents between saints

and *orixás*, we may speak of syncretism. From the point of view of the individual believer, on the other hand, the term 'pluralism' describes more exactly a situation in which two cults are practised on different occasions. In this context the French sociologist Roger Bastide, a specialist on Afro-Brazilian culture, put forward what he called the 'principle of compartmentalization' ('principe de coupure'), noting that Brazilians of African descent were more African in their religious practice than in other domains (he also used the term 'compartiments').[147]

There is an obvious analogy between this idea and the linguists' concept of 'code-switching', describing bilingual people shifting between one language and another in different situations. However, linguists also note a process that they describe as 'interference': bilinguals are generally unable to maintain a complete separation or segregation between their two languages, which in practice often influence or contaminate each other. In other words, generalizing the point, we may suggest that pluralism encourages the process of hybridization.

Traditions of appropriation

In the second place, it may be illuminating to distinguish between cultures with strong or weak traditions of appropriation and adaptation (in other words, traditions of modifying traditions). Hindu culture, for instance, has a greater propensity to incorporate alien elements than (say) Islamic culture. Japan offers another classic example of a tradition of appropriation. From the middle of the nineteenth century until the present, the Japanese have been borrowing cultural items from the West with apparent facility: the parliamentary system from England, the university system and the army from Germany, and much of their material culture from the United States. The speed with which the Japanese began to borrow in this way after 1850 would be scarcely intelligible if it had not followed a long tradition.

The Japanese had already borrowed and adapted many cultural traditions between the eighth and the eighteenth centuries, especially from China. They adopted Buddhism in its Chinese rather than its Indian form. They adopted the Chinese writing system, despite the contrast between Chinese, an uninflected language, and Japanese, a language that is full of inflections.[148] Even the imperial system of government was originally borrowed from China, although it was modified in important respects after the rise of the samurai and the shogun in the twelfth century.

When Westerners first made contact with Japan, in the sixteenth century, they discovered a culture in which

71

people were unusually interested in new ideas and new artefacts, from Christianity to firearms. We might therefore describe Japan as having an 'open' tradition, despite the notorious attempt by the government to close the country in the early seventeenth century and to cut it off from foreign influences (the Spaniards were expelled in 1624, and the Portuguese in 1638). This closure, isolation or 'seclusion' (known in Japanese as *sakoku*) was actually a reaction to the rapid spread of Christianity in Japan.

Like whole cultures, there are specific locales that are particularly favourable to cultural exchange, especially the metropolis and the frontier.

The metropolis and the frontier

Encounters between cultures, more exactly encounters between people from different cultures, or people from one culture and things from another, are obviously more intense in some places than others, 'contact zones' as they have been called.[149] Whenever cultural exchange takes place we may speak metaphorically of a 'trading zone', as the historian of science Peter Galison does in a study of what he calls the 'subcultures' of twentieth-century physics, describing these zones as spaces in which 'two dissimilar groups can find common ground', exchanging items of information while disagreeing about the wider significance of what is exchanged.[150] The point that exchange may have different meanings for different parties involved is an important one that recurs in other fields of research, notably in the study of religious conversion, as in the case of the 'working misunderstanding' discussed above.

It is also useful to consider locales or sites in a more literal sense of these terms. One major site of exchange is the metropolis, the cross-roads of both trade and culture, where people of diverse origins meet and interact. New York, London, Lagos, Los Angeles, Bombay-Mumbai and São Paulo are obvious contemporary examples. To return to the Middle Ages for a moment, in order to explain the hybrid architectural style of buildings in the city of L'viv, described above, we need to realize the importance of that city as an intermediary in the trade between Western Europe and the Black Sea region.

The importance of ports as sites of cultural encounter is striking – fifteenth-century Venice, sixteenth-century Lisbon and Seville, seventeenth-century Amsterdam, and so on. In the seventeenth and eighteenth centuries, the ports of Nagasaki and Canton (Guangzhou) were key locales of cultural exchange between Europe and Asia. Even in an age of air travel, the importance of twentieth-century New Orleans and Liverpool as meeting-places of

European and African musical traditions will be obvious enough.

What made and continues to make the metropolis an important site of cultural exchange is the presence of different groups of immigrants. Renaissance Venice was a home for Germans, Greeks, Jews, Slavs (mainly from the Dalmatian coast) and Turks. Early modern Lisbon had its minorities of French, Germans, Spaniards (generally Galicians) and Africans. Seventeenth-century Amsterdam had its southern Netherlanders, Germans, Scandinavians, Jews and Turks. Eighteenth-century St Petersburg had its Finns, Tatars, Germans, Jews, Swedes, Italians, and so on, while in eighteenth-century Calcutta it was possible to hear not only Bengali, Hindustani, Persian and English, but Portuguese, Arabic and Armenian as well.

Like immigrants today in London or Paris, New York or Los Angeles, these groups often tried to keep themselves to themselves, to work together, to marry within the group, to live in a particular quarter of the city – a sort of urban village – and to maintain their language and thus their original identity. Despite these attempts, most of the groups mentioned above were gradually assimilated into the local urban culture, each of them adding something new to the mix. For this reason, some scholars now speak of 'mestizo cities'.[151]

Urban languages sometimes illustrate the point vividly:

Bombay street language has recently been described as 'a mix of Hindi, Marathi and English, with snatches of Tamil and Gujarati thrown in'.[152] One might describe this language as 'Bombay mix', borrowing the English name for *chevda*, a spicy snack containing lentils, peanuts and noodles made from chickpea flour. The name has already been appropriated to describe a style of music.

Another locale favouring exchange and hybridization is the frontier. A famous example of a cultural frontier is the borderland between Christendom and Islam in Eastern Europe. In the sixteenth and seventeenth centuries, Polish or Hungarian nobles regularly fought the Turks and they may have hated the Turks. All the same, to their Western neighbours they looked rather like Turks, since they wore kaftans and used curved scimitars rather than the straight swords of Western tradition. These nobles defined themselves against the Turks by their Christianity, but they also defined themselves against Western Europeans by refusing to adopt their style of dress, or even by abandoning it, as the Poles did in the seventeenth century, and returning to their traditions, which were described at the time as 'Sarmatian' (some scholars then identified the Poles with the people of this name who moved from what is now Iran to Eastern Europe and threatened the Roman Empire).

Again, there was a common tradition of epic and

ballad on both sides of the Ottoman–Habsburg frontier, including stories and songs with the same heroes, such as Marko Kraljević, and the same battles between Christians and Muslims, although on one side of the border the Christians were presented as victorious and on the other side they were shown as defeated. In cases like these it seems reasonable to speak, like the leading Turkish historian Halil Inalcık, of a common culture of the frontier in contrast to that of the opposing centres, whether Istanbul or Vienna.[153]

Spain in the late Middle Ages was another such frontier area in which cultural exchanges between Christians, Jews and Moors in the domains of material culture and social practices, together with the hybrid productions that resulted, lasted for a long time and have been studied with unusual intensity, especially in the last few years.[154] Besides the buildings, including churches, that were decorated by Muslim craftsmen in the geometrical style generally associated with mosques, there are poems that switch from Spanish to Arabic and back again. Modern Spanish still contains many words of Arabic origin that entered the language in this period. Again, Spanish was sometimes written in Arabic script while Arabic texts might employ the Latin alphabet.[155]

These frontier zones, like cosmopolitan cities, may be described as 'intercultures', intersections between

cultures, in which the process of mixing ends in the creation of something new and distinctive, whether or not
we call this 'creole'.[156]

Classes as cultures

Concepts such as encounter, exchange and translation are
useful in discussions of interactions within a culture as
well as between cultures. It might be argued, for instance,
that in their famous studies of class, both Edward
Thompson (1924–93) and Pierre Bourdieu (1930–2002)
had too little to say about cultural interactions between
the middle class and the working class, whether these
interactions took the form of imitation or rejection.[157]
Take the example of the nobility and the bourgeoisie in
nineteenth-century Germany. It is well known that doctors, lawyers, professors, journalists and civil servants regularly fought duels at this time. For the sociologist
Norbert Elias (1897–1990), this phenomenon illustrates
the attraction that upper-class models exercised over the
middle class. It was one more instance of the trickle-down
effect in culture, the influence of the court on the wider
society that Elias liked to emphasize in other books of
his, reacting against the Marxist emphasis on market
forces in the making of modern culture.

For a younger German historian, on the other hand, middle-class duelling is evidence of the emancipation of the middle class, their increasing sense of their own worth. If she is right, then the duel offers us an excellent example of cultural appropriation and transformation, a case of the weapons characteristic of the nobility being neatly turned against them by some members of the bourgeoisie.[158] A problem remains. How, and on what grounds, can we decide between these rival interpretations?

In any case, it is interesting to note that the rise of cultural history, or of a cultural approach to history in general, has been accompanied by the appropriation of the word 'class', the traditional keyword in social analysis, for the study of culture.[159]

Varieties of response

Exchange is a consequence of encounters; but what are the consequences of exchange? It may be useful to distinguish four possible strategies, models or scenarios of response to cultural 'imports' or 'invasions'. These responses, all of them well-documented, are acceptance, especially the fashion for the foreign; rejection, which takes the forms of both resistance and purification; segregation; and adaptation.

The fashion for the foreign

The first possible strategy is that of acceptance or even welcome. The extreme case is that of the fashion for the foreign. Italophilia in the age of the Renaissance, for example, was followed in the seventeenth century by Francophilia and in the eighteenth and nineteenth centuries by 'Anglomania', an enthusiasm that spread from France, Italy and Germany to Russia and Brazil.[160]

More generally, an important part of the cultural

history of the world in the nineteenth and twentieth centuries might be written in terms of 'Westernization', including the fashion for the foreign in Russia, the Ottoman Empire, Japan, China and so many other countries, as well as reactions against this fashion. It is of course necessary to identify the groups or individuals who were most committed to the movement, and also their different motives for adherence, from the desire to fight the West with its own weapons – literally as well as metaphorically in the case of Peter the Great and the Young Turks – to the need for a younger generation to rebel against its elders.[161]

In Brazil, for instance, the journalist-priest Padre Miguel Lopes Gama (1791–1852) was already criticizing what he called the 'Londonization' of culture in the early nineteenth century.[162] The European suits worn by upper-class males in Rio de Janeiro in the nineteenth century offer a vivid example of the fashion for the foreign. Men sweated in woollen clothes at temperatures of 40 degrees in order to show that they were a leisure class exempt from physical work, to distinguish themselves from ordinary people, and above all to demonstrate their commitment to the 'civilized' values of the temperate zone. 'Anglomania' was extended to politics and the imitation of the British Parliament, despite what the Brazilian critic Roberto Schwartz has called 'the disparity between Brazilian society, based on slavery, and the ideas of European liberalism', leading him to coin the now famous phrase 'misplaced ideas'.[163]

These fashions deserve to be taken seriously by cultural historians, in the sense of being analysed and explained as well as described. The appeal of Italian styles in other parts of Europe in the sixteenth century, like the appeal of American styles in the twentieth century, was in part at least a recognition that Italians were more rapid and more creative in responding to social changes which were taking place in Europe as a whole, so that, in Florence in particular (in the USA in the 1950s), one might have said that 'tomorrow is already here'.

However, the tendency to assume that cultural exchange is always a reflection of tolerance and open-mindedness is one that historians should resist. It should not be forgotten that cultural interaction in late medieval Spain, the so-called *convivencia*, took place at a time of pogroms, forced conversions, and inquisitors hunting down *moriscos* and *marranos*, crypto-Muslims and crypto-Jews. In other words, cultural 'harmony', or at any rate appropriation, was apparently combined with social disharmony, especially after 1348, when the trauma of the Black Death led to a hunt for scapegoats who could be made to bear the blame for the disaster.[164] A similar point might be made about the Polish and Hungarian nobles, mentioned earlier, and their appropriations of items of culture from their Muslim neighbours.

How can this combination of harmony and conflict be explained? The crucial question, easy to ask but difficult to answer, is the question of meaning. It is quite possible that what historians now view as a common heritage might have been perceived by Christians and Muslims alike as really 'theirs' alone. Local Christians in Spain or Poland may have simply forgotten that other Christians associated geometrical decoration or the use of the scimitar with Islam. In similar fashion, Greeks who object to the term 'Turkish coffee' today have chosen to forget a well-known historical fact, that coffee-making originated in the Islamic world (in Yemen in the fifteenth century) and radiated outwards from Istanbul.

Resistance

The problems raised by borrowing lead us to a second possible strategy; the strategy of resistance, defending the cultural frontiers against invasion.[165]

Cultural identities are often defined by opposition, as a shrewd English traveller to Russia, the physician Samuel Collins, had already pointed out in the seventeenth century, long before Lévi-Strauss emphasized the importance of binary thinking: 'Because the Roman Catholics kneel at their devotion, they [the Russians] will stand ... Because the Polonians [the Poles] shave their beards, they count it sinful to cut them. Because the Tartar abhors swine's flesh, they eat it rather than any other flesh.'[166]

In the Renaissance, the Italophilia visible among the elites of many European countries produced its opposite, a wave of Italophobia. In Spain, for instance, the poets Garcilaso de la Vega and Joán Boscán were criticized because they wrote in the Italian style, abandoning the native tradition. In Portugal, Francisco de Holanda was described as the devil in Italian dress.[167]

In the seventeenth century it was the turn of the French to become the target of angry 'nativists' who were defending the purity of local traditions. In Germany, for instance, the critique of the invasion of the language by French words, especially in the domain of good behaviour (*compliment*, *galant*, *mode*, etc.), was particularly intense in the middle decades of the century. Language societies were founded with the defence of the purity of the language as one of their main ideals. The linguistic campaign was part of a more general reaction against foreign cultural models, from clothes to cuisine – the 'imitation of the French' ('Nachahmung der Französen') denounced by the philosopher Christian Thomasius (1655–1728).[168] Just as some cultures are unusually receptive to ideas or artefacts from outside, others are unusually resistant, as a pair of examples from Africa may suggest. The Igbo of Nigeria, the ethnic group of a number of leading African novelists (including Chinua Achebe, discussed above) are, like the Brazilians and the Japanese, well known for welcoming the unfamiliar. By contrast, the Pakot, who come from West Kenya, are notorious for their resistance to change and their attachment to their own traditions.[169] It may be instructive to ask which European or Asian cultures most resemble the Pakot.

For some periods of its history, 'Spain' might be an appropriate answer to this question, at least after the expulsion of Jews and Muslims in 1492. In the middle of the sixteenth century, there was an official attempt to close the country, not unlike the Japanese *sakoku* discussed above. From 1558, individuals who imported foreign books without official permission became liable to the death penalty. In 1559, Philip II forbade Spaniards to study abroad except in Bologna, Rome and Naples (even the University of Padua was regarded as dangerous, perhaps because of its proximity to Venice, widely regarded as a centre of liberty and licence). The Index of Prohibited Books published in Spain was more severe than the Roman Index that was binding on the whole Church. Thus the *Essays* of Michel de Montaigne (1533–92) were placed on the Spanish Index in 1640, but on the Roman Index only in 1676.

The contrast between late medieval Spain, the great age of the coexistence and interaction between three cultures, Christian, Muslim and Jewish (famously described by Américo Castro), and the same country in the seventeenth and eighteenth centuries is indeed a striking one, suggesting that – as in the case of Christianity in Japan – it may have been precisely the open-mindedness or cultural receptivity of ordinary people that led the authorities to take repressive action.[170]

As a result of the policy of *sakoku*, from the 1630s to the 1860s Japanese culture was a 'world within walls', as the American literary historian Donald Keene has famously called it, so that 'the literature of this time developed largely without reference to foreign examples'.[171] It should be added that isolation did not stifle creativity. This period, especially the so-called 'Genroku Era' (1688–1704), was a golden age of Japanese literature, including the novels and stories of Iharu Saikaku (1642–93) and the plays of Chikamatsu Monzaemon (1653–1725).

Other possible parallels to the Pakot include two remarkable cases of cultural resistance – especially remarkable for believers in technological progress – the Muslim rejection of print and the Japanese rejection of the gun.

In the case of print, it has been plausibly argued that the essential reason for resistance was the threat posed by the new, foreign medium of communication to the traditional Islamic system for the transmission of knowledge, which was essentially a person-to-person system.[172] After all, the great Islamic empires of the early modern world – the Ottoman, Persian and Mughal empires – did not resist all forms of Western innovation. They adopted firearms with enthusiasm, so much so that they have been described as 'gunpowder empires'. Print, on the other hand, was viewed as less of a tool and more of a threat.

The Japanese too, notably the military leader Oda Nobunaga (1534–82), were enthusiastic for guns when they first encountered these artefacts in the sixteenth century. Indeed, Nobunaga ordered 500 guns for his army. All the same, the new technology was rejected in the seventeenth century, because the ruling military class, the samurai, saw it as incompatible with their ethos. Swords seem to have had an even greater symbolic value for the samurai than they did for medieval knights.[173]

The contrast between open and closed traditions raises an intriguing problem, that of explaining differences in receptivity.[174] Is it, for example, the well-integrated culture that is relatively closed, while the culture open to ideas from outside is divided? Or is the fundamental question one of self-confidence? When people are confident of the superiority of their culture, they often take little interest in foreign ideas. In the case of the Ottoman Empire, for instance, defeats in the late seventeenth century seem to have encouraged the ruling elite to take the West more seriously than before. There seem to be favourable and unfavourable moments for cultural exchange.

We should not forget, however, that what we call 'cultures' are not homogeneous but heterogeneous and that different groups within them may react in very different ways to cultural encounters. In some cases, the question of borrowing became a matter of debate.

In nineteenth-century Russia, for instance, the movement of Westernization was resisted from the 1840s onwards by the so-called 'Slavophils', who insisted that foreign ideas were 'out of place' in their country, alien to its traditions, incapable of taking root in its soil. In fact, the Russian critique of slavish imitation was older than that. The journalist-publisher Nikolai Novikov (1744–1818), for instance, criticized his contemporaries for having 'become accustomed to adopting greedily everything from foreigners'.[175] The philosopher Petr Chaadaev (1794–1856) argued that the Russians were out of place, living between the worlds of the West and the East like nomads, while their own culture was 'based wholly upon importation and imitation'. He made this denunciation in a *Lettre philosophique* (1836) which was, ironically enough, written in French.[176]

The Brazilian writer Euclides da Cunha was reacting in a similar way to the Slavophils when he denounced his own culture, as we have seen, as 'a culture of borrowing' blindly or mechanically copying what in other nations was an organic growth.[177]

Cultural purification

Reactions against the fashion for the foreign have often taken the extreme form of movements for purification, including what is now known as 'ethnic cleansing'. Refusal to borrow is combined with attempts to root out what has already been borrowed and assimilated, a kind of 'dehybridization'.

In the case of language, for example, a movement to return to pure 'Attic' Greek began in the late classical period in response to what was perceived as an invasion of the language by foreign words.[178] Again, the Protestant humanist-printer Henri Estienne denounced the italianate 'jargon' of the French court in the 1570s as vehemently as the French government continues to denounce *franglais*.[179]

In Germany, the preoccupation with linguistic purity, mentioned above, reached its peak early in the twentieth century. Already, in 1885, a society for the defence of German had been founded, the Allgemein Deutsche Sprachverein, with its journal *Muttersprache*. The 1930s were the high point of the so-called *Fremdwortjagd*, the hunt for and replacement of foreign terms which had concealed themselves in the German language, French terms in particular. Thus a railway platform, once *Perron*, became *Bahnsteig*, *Universität* turned into *Althochschule*, and so on. This programme was much older than Nazi ideals of *Deutschtum* ('Germanity') and cultural purification, but it harmonized with them. Hence the Nazis supported the Sprachverein at first, although they ended the hunt in 1940 after one linguist had been rash enough to criticize the language of the Führer.[180] Since that time the purists have been relatively quiet in Germany, perhaps because purism is associated with Nazism. Indeed, the German language has become extremely hospitable to American imports.

In France, on the other hand, this form of linguistic xenophobia became important at the very moment that it was declining in Germany, after the Second World War. *Franglais* is the linguistic aspect of what the French used to call 'the American challenge', *le défi américain*. The response to this challenge has been purification. General de

Gaulle, for instance, found time between the Algerian cri-
sis and the events of May 1968 to set up a committee for
defence of the French language. In 1975, the Bas-Lauriol
law was passed, prohibiting the use of a foreign word (at
least by government departments) whenever a French word
with the same meaning was already in circulation. Whatever the French do informally, this official policy continues.

Cultural segregation

A third possible strategy or conscious reaction to a cultural invasion is that of segregation. In this case, the line
is drawn not between the self and the other but inside
the home culture, renouncing the idea of defending the
whole territory in order to concentrate on keeping part of
it free from contamination by foreign influences.

There have long been groups for whom the indis-
criminate acceptance of the foreign and the undiscrimi-
nating rejection of borrowing seemed equally absurd. In
the nineteenth and twentieth centuries, the Turks and the
Chinese, among others, wanted to borrow Western technology without accepting Western values. For example,
the Young Ottomans criticized the government of Fuad
Pasha (1815–69) for thinking Westernization equivalent
to what one of them described as 'the establishment of

theatres, frequenting ball-rooms, being liberal about the infidelities of one's wife and using toilets'. What was needed, according to them, was Western artillery or engineering.[181]

Japan in the second half of the nineteenth century offers another famous instance of cultural segregation. At this time, some upper-class men, at least, began to live what has been called a 'double life', a life both Western and traditional, consuming two kinds of food according to the occasion, wearing two kinds of clothes (a kimono at home, for example, and a Western suit at the office), reading books in two kinds of script and living in traditional houses that now included a room furnished in the Western style[182] Segregation of this kind continues today, although the Western room in a Japanese-style apartment has gradually been replaced by the Japanese room in a Western-style apartment.

In similar fashion, Gilberto Freyre described some nineteenth-century Brazilians wearing a cashmere jacket and a tie in the street, but a traditional linen jacket in their own house. Again, in his discussion of the Santidade de Jaguaripe, mentioned earlier, the Brazilian historian Ronaldo Vainfas speaks not of true syncretism in the sense of the fusion of beliefs from different sources, but rather of what he calls 'cultural disjunction' and a double life split between the pagan and Christian worlds.[183] The

Brazilian tradition of religious pluralism discussed above seems to go back a long way.

Another type of segregation is often to be seen in the large polyglot and multiethnic cities, past and present, described above as contact zones. Viewed at close quarters, these cities often resemble cultural mosaics, composed of very different pieces, and the phrase 'urban mosaic' has even passed into ordinary language, at least in the USA. However, the cultural segregation of immigrants must not be exaggerated. It varies with their original culture, with the urban environment within which they are trying to establish themselves, and also with age, since older people find it difficult to learn a new language and are less likely to take up an occupation that would take them out of their urban 'village'. What commonly happens is that many individuals, especially younger men, live a double life in the Japanese sense of the term, part of it passed in the host culture during the working day and another part in their traditional culture in their hours of leisure.

Curiously enough, there seem to be few studies so far of the breakdown of cultural segregation in the second or third generation, with bilingualism, mixed marriages and later assimilation. It is known, for example, that the French Protestants who left France in the late seventeenth century and settled in Amsterdam, London and Berlin attended their own churches and continued to publish books in French, but the decline of this cultural segregation remains to be studied. It is also worth noting that, in certain domains, such as cuisine, and in some groups (the Poles for instance, who continue to speak their own language in England or the USA), the traditions of the immigrants survive better than others. Over the generations, though, segregation merges into adaptation.

Adaptation

A common response to an encounter with another culture, or items from another culture, is adaptation, or borrowing piecemeal in order to incorporate the pieces into a traditional structure. This is what the French anthropologist Claude Lévi-Strauss called 'bricolage' and claimed to be a feature of what he called 'wild thought' ('la pensée sauvage'). More recently, this process of appropriation and re-employment has been described and analysed in the case of Western culture as well, notably by Michel de Certeau in a famous study of the French working class in the 1970s.[184]

Cultural adaptation may be analysed as a double movement of de-contextualization and re-contextualization, lifting an item out of its original setting and modifying it to fit its new environment. The process of 'tropicalization' so often discussed and so tirelessly advocated by the Brazilian intellectual Gilberto Freyre in so many domains, from architecture to cooking, makes a good example of the process, although it is necessary to distinguish different kinds of adaptation.

Tropicalization in the literal sense of the term occurs when clothes or houses designed with cold countries in mind are modified when they are exported to hot countries. A famous yet controversial example comes from the architecture of Lúcio Costa (1902–98) and Oscar Niemeyer (1907–), sometimes described as a successful adaptation of the ideas and designs of Le Corbusier to the Brazilian environment, and sometimes criticized on the grounds that the process of adaptation did not go far enough. On the other hand, if wooden chairs of English design changed their shape when they were copied in Brazil (above, p. 15), the modifications may have been less deliberate, whether they were a result of the shift from English wood (walnut, for instance) to Brazilian woods (such as jacaranda) or of differences in local craft traditions.

Long-distance trade, especially the trade between Europe and Asia in the early modern period, offers other fascinating instances of cultural interaction and hybridization. In the case of textiles, a famous example is that of chintz, a printed cloth produced in India for export to Europe. The printed designs combined Persian, Indian and Chinese motifs and followed patterns which were sent to India by the directors of the Dutch and English East India Companies. In other words, these textiles were produced in a generalized 'oriental' style which should be regarded as a joint Eurasian production.[185]

Again, a great deal of Chinese and Japanese porcelain was exported to Europe in the seventeenth and eighteenth centuries (70 million pieces, according to one calculation). Once again the intermediaries were the East India Companies, and once again traditional designs were gradually modified to suit the taste of Western customers. The famous 'willow pattern' plates so popular in Britain to this day are an example of such modifications. It has been suggested that porcelain was 'the principal material vehicle for the assimilation and transmission of cultural themes across immense distances'.[186]

On one side, then, we find Asian artists imitating European styles or, at the very least, choosing from the local repertoire the elements that had been proved to appeal to Western customers. On the other side, we find European artists imitating Asian styles and the rise of the fashion for the exotic. The eighteenth-century European craze for Chinoiserie is well known, but already in the sixteenth century, Genoese craftsmen were imitating Ming porcelain.[187] On occasion it is virtually impossible to say whether a given artefact is the work of Asianizing Europeans or Europeanizing Asians.

The points that deserve to be emphasized here are: first, the different stages in the process; second, the number of different people involved in it; and third, the fact that changes take place on both sides. The metaphor of cultural 'negotiation', discussed earlier in this volume, seems to be a particularly useful one in the analysis of processes of this kind.

Circularity

The metaphor of the circle is also useful to refer to adaptations of foreign items of culture that are so thorough that the result can sometimes be 're-exported' successfully to the place from which the item originated. Take the example of circularity between the domains of the sacred and the profane. In early Christian times, the Church appropriated themes from the official rhetoric and iconography of the Roman Empire, with God or Christ in the place of the Emperor, while in early modern Europe, the state sometimes re-appropriated these themes. Some of Louis XIV's contemporaries thought that the King had committed blasphemy by allowing lights to be lit in front of his statue in Paris, as if he were a saint. Yet it might be argued that, in allowing this kind of veneration, Louis was simply returning to ancient Roman political practice.[188]

Another kind of circularity is that between 'High' (or learned) and 'Low' (or popular) culture. Today, exchanges between these two cultures have become well known and even fashionable, so it may be worth pointing out that they also occurred earlier. Writers from the upper classes such as Ariosto, Rabelais, Shakespeare and Cervantes all drew on the popular culture of their own day for inspiration, but their own works returned to the people, sometimes in simplified form.[189]

The history of the cultural relations between Japan and the West in the nineteenth and twentieth centuries offers a number of fascinating examples of this kind of circularity. In the visual arts, for instance, the Japanese discovery of the Impressionists follows a slightly earlier discovery, by Edouard Manet, Claude Monet and others, of the art of Japan. The example of Japan encouraged Western artists, already in revolt against their own academic traditions, to imitate the asymmetrical compositions, calligraphic lines and the use of flat patches of colour to be found in woodblock prints in particular.[190] Again, the American philosopher Ernest Fenollosa (1853–1908), who arrived in Japan in 1878 to teach at the Imperial University, became an enthusiast for traditional Japanese art. In so doing, strange as it may seem, he influenced Japanese artists such as Hogai and Gaho.

In music, Japanese composers such as Tōru Takemitsu (1930–96) have been influenced by Western composers such as John Cage (1912–92) and Pierre Boulez (1925–) who had already been influenced by the music of Japan. Giacomo Puccini (1858–1924) drew on Japanese music for his *Madama Butterfly* (1907), while the Japanese have in turn adapted Puccini in a series of what a recent historian has called 'repatriations'.[191] In the case of the cinema, one may be entitled to suspect that the samurai films of Akira Kurosawa (1910–98) and other Japanese directors owe something to the tradition of the American Western. If so, the compliment was returned when John Sturges made *The Magnificent Seven* (1960), a 'translation' of Kurosawa's famous *Seven Samurai* (1954).

One British writer who was a success in nineteenth-century Japan was the Scotsman Samuel Smiles (1812–1904), author of *Self-Help* (1859), a collection of success stories about individuals who went from rags to riches, thanks to their own effort and intelligence. The success of this book may suggest that the Japanese had been converted to Victorian values. However, there were local precedents for this kind of story. In the seventeenth century, the popular writer Iharu Saikaku had already published *The Eternal Storehouse of Japan*, a collection of stories about enterprising and hard-working townspeople who were rewarded with riches.

Again, the Irish poet William Butler Yeats (1865–1939) wrote a play, *At the Hawk's Well* (1917), in the style of the traditional *Nō* dramas of Japan, although his own play was set in the Irish 'heroic age' and may therefore be described as a hybrid of East and West. The Japanese tradition interested Yeats because the use of masks and dancers offered him a means of breaking with the traditions of the 'realist' theatre of his time. A Japanese writer, Yokomichi Mario, in turn adapted *At the Hawk's Well* as a *Nō* play, performed in Tokyo in 1949.[192]

These examples of circularity suggest that the culture of the West has helped modernizing Japanese to rediscover or revalue some of their own traditions. The combination of distance with similarity seems to be a key factor in the success of particular cultural exports or, shall we say, 'transplants'. We have returned to the question, evoked earlier, of congruences and convergences.

Translators

The example of *At the Hawk's Well* raises another topic that is central to any discussion of cultural encounters. Analyses of cultural hybridization often speak of general trends and ignore individuals. These analyses have probably got their priorities right, in the sense that trends are much larger than individuals. All the same, it always makes sense to ask: who does the adapting?

Take the example of translators between languages. Translators are often displaced people. In many cultures, interpreters have formed a distinctive group in which members of marginal communities were important. Relations between the Ottoman Empire and Western Europe, for instance, long depended on the services of Jews and Greeks as linguistic intermediaries.[193]

People who transferred their allegiance from one culture to another have often played an important role in the process of interpreting. A famous or notorious individual case is that of Doña Marina, 'La Malinche', the interpreter and the mistress of Hernán Cortés (1485–1547), conqueror of Mexico. Collective examples include the so-called 'renegades' who converted from Christianity to Islam, or the 'new Christians' (in other words, converted Jews) who interpreted for the Portuguese in South Asia.[194]

In Europe too, Renaissance translators from one language to another were often émigrés, exiles or refugees. They took advantage of their liminal position and made a career of mediating between the two countries to which they owed a kind of allegiance. It is likely that these people had a 'double consciousness' (above, p. 31), and that this double consciousness assisted them in the task of translation.[195]

Curiously enough, these European amphibians have been studied less intensively than their equivalents in the Americas and in Asia. For example, Greek refugees to Italy before and after the fall of Constantinople were responsible for some influential translations from ancient Greek into Latin. Again, Italian Protestant refugees, such as Celio Secundo Curione, Scipione Gentile, Francesco Negri, Silvestro Teglio and Giovanni Niccolò Stoppani, played an important role in the reception of the Renaissance in northern Europe. Gentile lived in Germany, while Curione, Negri, Stoppani and Teglio were all refugees in Switzerland. Besides religious works, they translated secular texts such as Niccolò Machiavelli's *Prince* (1560), Francesco Guicciardini's *History of Italy* (1566) and Tasso's *Jerusalem Delivered* (1584).

A famous example from England is that of John Florio (1553–1625) – whose hybrid name expresses a hybrid identity – who came from an Italian Protestant family who moved to England to escape persecution. He made his living by giving lessons in Italian, and compiled an English–Italian dictionary, as well as making his now famous translation of the essays of Montaigne from French into English.[196]

FIVE

Varieties of outcome

Still to be discussed are the outcomes or consequences of cultural interaction over the long term. From this point onwards I shall be speaking less as a cultural historian and more as an individual concerned like so many of us with the fate of world cultures in our age of accelerating globalization, choosing examples from the past in order to comment on possible futures. Where the last chapter concentrated on conscious reactions and deliberate strategies, this one is more concerned with what is likely to happen independently of the intentions, desires or expectations of individuals and groups.

One possibility will be mentioned only to reject it, and that is the continued existence of independent cultures. In our world, no culture is an island. Indeed, as the epigraphs to this volume suggest, it is a very long time since most cultures were islands. It has become more and more difficult over the centuries to maintain what might be called the 'insulation' of cultures in order to defend this kind of insularity.

In other words, all cultural traditions are now in more

or less direct contact with alternative traditions. Segregation is a possibility over the short term, as we have seen, but examples such as that of the French Protestant exiles or the modern Japanese suggest that it is not a viable option over *la longue durée*. Traditions are like building sites, under constant construction or reconstruction, whether the individuals and groups who participate in those traditions realize this or not.

Take the case of Candomblé, discussed earlier and interpreted in a brilliant essay by the French sociologist Roger Bastide as the symbolic reconstruction of African space, a kind of psychological compensation to Afro-Brazilians for the loss of their homeland.[197] All the same, it has been shown that the practices of Candomblé have gradually changed in the course of time. Hence it cannot be said that Candomblé is 'pure' while Umbanda (discussed above) is a hybrid.[198] It is safe to say that African traditions are more important in Candomblé than in Umbanda, but both forms have been hybridized or translated.

If independence and segregation are both eliminated, there still remain four main possibilities or scenarios for the future of the cultures of our planet. In the first place, homogenization, the meltdown of different cultures, a consequence of globalization that many people today both expect and fear. In the second place, resistance or 'counter-globalization'. Thirdly, what might be called 'cultural diglossia', a combination of global with local cultures. In the fourth place, the rise of new syntheses. Let me discuss these four scenarios in order.

Cultural homogenization

The first scenario is that of cultural homogenization, whether its coming is predicted for 2050, 2100 or even later. Those who dislike the trend often speak of the 'Americanization' of culture or of the 'Coca-Cola effect' (the overtones of Americanophobia are reminiscent of the Italophobia and the Francophobia discussed earlier). The hostile critics fear the loss of a sense of place, indeed the loss of place itself, re-placed by the proliferation of 'non-places' such as airports.[199] Faced with the scenario of hybridization, they might reply that the mixing of all cultures in a global pot is a stage in their eventual homogenization.

We certainly see many signs of a rise of a global, quasi-global, or at least increasingly global culture, expecially in the West but also in Japan, and increasingly in China as well. Take the case of contemporary art. We do not see a simple homogenization in the sense of the rise of a single style at the expense of all its competitors. What we do see is a more complex homogenization in the sense of a variety of competing styles, abstract and representational, op and pop, and so on, all of which are now available to artists virtually irrespective of the place in which they happen to live. At a local level, there is heterogenization. At an individual level, there is more choice, more freedom, a widening of options. At a global level, though, what we see is the reverse, a narrowing of diversity.

In other arts, we are witnessing another kind of homogenization. Thanks to the growth of a global market, some writers, like some directors of films 'consciously or unconsciously build translatability into their art forms'.[200] In the case of films, Hollywood aims at a global market, and in Europe too co-productions across national frontiers have become more and more common since the 1960s. Michelangelo Antonioni (1912–2007), for instance, who established his reputation with films made in Italian in Italy with Italian actors, turned to working with an international cast and international finance to make films in English such as *Blow-Up* (1967) and *Zabriskie Point* (1969).

In the case of the novel, a recent interview with Milan Kundera (1929–) which I happened, in this global age, to read in translation in a Brazilian newspaper, is surely revealing of a wider trend. Before 1968, Kundera lived in Prague and wrote in Czech, primarily for a Czech public. He now lives in Paris, writes in French and writes, so he explains in the interview, primarily for a world public. In important ways that have not, so far as I know, been analysed either in detail or in depth, privileging a global rather than a local public changes the work itself in all sorts of ways. Kundera's novels certainly changed after 1968. They became less social and more metaphysical, with fewer local references and more reflections on the human condition.

A similar point might be made about other forms of cultural production, including histories. I can testify that, as I have gradually become accustomed to the idea that my books might be translated into various languages, I have tried in one study after another (including this one) to avoid allusions that would not be easily intelligible outside Britain, or even outside Europe. I have started to think in terms of a potentially global audience, wondering whether a particular statement or allusion will be clear to Japanese or to Brazilian readers. In the process I seem to be reconstructing myself as more of a world citizen, and I am sure that I am not alone in this.

These changes are surely inevitable, but they do not take us very close to the scenario of full homogenization. The power of misunderstanding – or shall we say, unconscious reinterpretation – should not be underestimated. Even if people in all the regions of the world viewed identical images on their television screens at the same time, they would not 'read' or understand what they saw in the same way. This point emerges very clearly from empirical studies of the reception of the soap opera *Dallas* in different countries, from Israel to Fiji. Russian emigrants to Israel, for instance, viewed *Dallas* as a satire on capitalism.[201]

It should be added that historians are becoming less and less convinced that movements of homogenization were successful in the past. They used to believe that processes such as Hellenization, Romanization, Hispanization, Anglicization and so on were essentially victorious. Today, however, there is a strong tendency to deny this success – to argue, for instance, that the Romans never penetrated deep into the culture of different parts of their empire. Again, the subordinate or 'submerged' cultures of Latin America, New Zealand, China and even Japan (long thought to be an exemplary instance of cultural unity) are now receiving increasing attention at a time when there is an ethnic awakening, a kind of 'return of the repressed'. Is there any reason to think that globalization will be any different?

It is surely revealing that supporters of the homogenization thesis – whether they love or hate what they describe – usually draw on a restricted range of examples, from convenience food and drink to the design of airports. Homogenizers often fail to take into account the creativity of reception and the renegotiation of meanings discussed earlier, or the importance of the narcissism of minor differences, discussed below. Even their favourite example of Coca-Cola has been brilliantly re-interpreted by the anthropologist Daniel Miller in an analysis of what he calls 'the local contextualization of a global form' in Trinidad.[202] As we have seen, the global spread of McDonald's has been described in similar terms.

The vision of everyone in 2050, say, speaking English – like a foreigner, of course – and watching the same television programmes at the same time is an obvious caricature. Major world languages such as Chinese, Arabic and Spanish, not to mention French, Portuguese and Russian, still have a good deal of life left in them. And so do the major world religions, even if they are now influencing one another more than ever before, as the circulation of terms like 'Zen Catholicism' or 'Zen Judaism' suggest.[203]

Counter-globalization

Today, we see a good deal of resistance to the 'intrusion' or 'invasion' of global forms of culture. This is scarcely surprising. The reaction is a case of what sociologists sometimes call 'cultural lag'. As the French historian Fernand Braudel used to emphasize, different kinds of change take place at different speeds.

The linked changes which we currently describe as 'globalization' are primarily technological and economic. Technology, especially the technology of communication, now moves so fast as to leave most of us dizzy. Institutions lag behind, despite the need to adapt them to the changing world. Still slower are changes in human attitudes, especially those fundamental attitudes or unspoken assumptions which – following French historians once again – I shall describe as 'mentalities'. What might be called the 'resilience' of traditional local mentalities should not be underestimated. Changes in mentalities are necessarily slow, given the importance of the first two or three years of life for the future development of each individual. The fundamental values of the generation that will be old in 2080 have already been instilled.

No wonder then that in many parts of the world there are reactions against cultural globalization. For convenience, let us speak of 'counter-globalization'. Education can be and indeed is used to support cultural resistance of this kind (courses in local history, compulsory lessons in Irish or Basque, and so on).

In this scenario an important role is played by the collective phenomenon of the revolt of the regions, already described in the sixties by the Occitan intellectual Robert Lafont (1923–) and others as the 'regionalist revolution'.[204] From our point of view, it does not matter whether a given movement – Breton, say, or Catalan – uses the language of region or nation – or indeed that of religion, as in the case of Serbia or Bosnia. The point is the stress on local culture and local identity, whether it takes the form of the revival of dying languages, ethnic cleansing or smashing the windows of McDonald's, as happened in Millau, in the south of France, in 1999.

Freud had a good phrase for what we see happening in so many parts of the globe: the 'narcissism of minor differences'.[205] A topical example – but one with a long history – is that of Catholics and Protestants in Northern Ireland, two groups that share the same territory and have so much of their culture in common that it is difficult for outsiders to distinguish them. Nevertheless, they persist – a minority on each side persists, at any rate – in treating each other as the Other, the opposite of the self.

The Dutch anthropologist Anton Blok, agreeing with Freud, adds the point that it is the threat of the loss of traditional identities that triggers the narcissism, often accompanied by violence against the Other.[206] The English anthropologist Anthony Cohen makes a similar point: 'the symbolic expression of community and its boundaries increases in importance as the actual geo-social boundaries of the community are undermined, blurred or otherwise weakened'.[207]

In other words, this is a powerful reaction but one that

may not last for many more decades. Resistance is doomed to ultimate failure in the sense that the aims of the resisters, to halt the march of history or to bring back the past, are unattainable. Yet resistance is not futile, because the actions of the resisters, like that of other losers in history, will have an effect on the cultures of the future. It may not be the effect they desired, but it will be an effect all the same.

Cultural diglossia

A third possibility is that in a future world of global culture, we may all become bicultural, living a double life like the Japanese who were described in an earlier section of this volume. We will all speak EFL ('English as a Foreign Language') or another world language (Chinese, Spanish, Arabic) in some situations but retain our own local language or dialect in others, participating in world culture but retaining a local culture. I should like to call this outcome 'cultural diglossia' (following a model proposed by some sociolinguists a generation ago), rather than 'cultural bilingualism', because the two elements are not likely to be equal.[208]

As a description of the present of some of us and the near future of more of us, this scenario seems to me to be a highly plausible one. It is a milder version of the conscious cultural segregation that was discussed in an earlier section of this volume. There were and there still are many people who are able to switch between cultures as they do between languages or linguistic registers, choosing what they consider to be appropriate to the situation in which they find themselves. The implication that we are all immigrants now, whether we realize this or not, is one that deserves to be taken seriously, like Nestor Canclini's remark that the frontier is everywhere.[209]

Over the long term, on the other hand, we can safely predict that at least some of the divisions between spheres in the 'double life' will melt away. What might be described (from the purists' point of view) as 'contamination' is bound to occur, as has indeed happened in the case of Japan, as well as in that of the urban immigrants who were described above. Like national borders, the walls of the ghetto are not proof against cultural invasion or infiltration.

The creolization of the world

The idea that cultural encounters lead to cultural hybridity or mixing of some kind is, appropriately enough, a middle position between two views of the past, both of which may be criticized as superficial. On one side, there is the claim that a culture or a cultural tradition can remain 'pure'. On the other, we find the assertion that a single culture (the French in the past, the American in the present, or the global in the future) can conquer others completely.

Within the group of 'hybridizers', we may distinguish those with negative attitudes from those who view the trend more positively. On one side, the critics emphasize chaos, what Arnold Toynbee used to call 'cultural disintegration' and self-consciously post-modern analysts often describe as 'fragmentation'.[210] These critics emphasize what is being lost in the process of cultural change. It is difficult to deny that these losses occur. To return to Kundera for a moment, I happen to think that his finest novel is *The Joke* (1967), written in his Czech period and enriched, even for foreign readers, by its references to local culture. He paid a price for his emigration.

However, the critics of the hybridization process surely overlook its positive side, the tendency to synthesis and to the emergence of new forms. One illuminating way of analysing these tendencies is to work with the concept of 'creolization', introduced a few pages back. The point of introducing a relatively unfamiliar word into a debate in which, as we have seen, too many terms are already floating is to emphasize tendencies to synthesis, to the creation of what the American anthropologist Marshall

Sahlins (1930–) describes as the creation of a new 'cultural order', a cultural schema on a grand scale. In his studies of Hawaii before and after the encounter with Captain Cook, Sahlins outlines a dialectical theory of cultural change in which ideas, objects or practices from outside are absorbed or 'ordered' by a given culture, but in the process (once a certain critical threshold has been passed), the culture is 're-ordered'.[211]

Another metaphor that may be helpful is that of 'crystallization'. I use it here in order to suggest that when cultural encounters and exchanges take place, a period of relative fluidity ('freedom' if you approve of it, 'chaos' if you disapprove) is rapidly followed by a time when the fluid solidifies, congeals, turns into routine and becomes resistant to further change. Old elements have been arranged into a new pattern. To use the language of the sociologist Norbert Elias, there is a new 'figuration'. How the process works, to what extent crystallization and reconfiguration are unconscious and collective and how far they depend on creative individuals, is difficult, if not impossible, to say. All the same, this aspect of cultural exchange surely deserves emphasis, whether we are thinking about the past, the present or the future.

To sum up the last few paragraphs and make them relevant to the problem of the consequences of globalization, I should like, following the Swedish anthropologist

Ulf Hannerz and others, to suggest that we are now witnessing the emergence of a new form of cultural order.[212] This is a global cultural order, but one that – if Carl von Sydow, the theorist of oicotypes, is right – may quickly diversify by being adapted to different local environments. In other words, today's hybrid forms are not necessarily a stage on the way towards a homogeneous global culture.

We should not dismiss the uncomfortable insights of the theorists of homogenization or the critics of hybridity. It is possible that the balance between centrifugal and centripetal forces has finally tipped towards the latter. All the same, the analysis of our past, present and future culture or cultures that I find most convincing is the one that sees a new order coming into being, the formation of new oicotypes, the crystallization of new forms, the reconfiguration of cultures, the 'creolization of the world'.

1 Perry Anderson, *Origins of Post-Modernity* (London, 1998).

2 Marwan M. Kraidy, *Hybridity: Or the Cultural Logic of Globalization* (Philadelphia, 2005), 3.

3 Jean-Loup Amselle, *Logiques métisses* (1990: English trans., *Mestizo Logics: Anthropology of Identity in Africa and Elsewhere*, Stanford, 1998).

4 Jan Nederveen Pieterse, 'Globalization as Hybridization', *International Sociology* 9 (1994), 161–84, expanded version, *Globalization and Culture: Global Mélange* (Lanham, MD, 2004). Cf. Kraidy, *Hybridity*.

5 Georgina Born and David Hesmondhalgh (eds.), *Western Music and its Others* (Berkeley and Los Angeles, 2000).

6 Quoted in Chris Rojek, *Stuart Hall* (Cambridge, 2003), 49.

7 Ien Ang, *On Not Speaking Chinese: Living Between Asia and the West* (London, 2001), 3.

8 Edward Said, *Out of Place* (London, 2000); Nehru quoted in Robert J. C. Young, *Postcolonialism: An Historical Introduction* (Oxford, 2001), 348.

9 Nestor G. Canclini, *Culturas híbridas: estrategias para entrar y salir de la modernidad* (1992: English trans., *Hybrid Cultures: Strategies for Entering and Leaving Modernity*, Minneapolis, 1995); Eduardo Archetti, *Masculinities: Football, Polo and Tango in Argentina* (Oxford, 1999).

10 José Vasconcelos, *La raza cósmica* (1929: English trans., *The Cosmic*

Race, Baltimore, 1997); Gilberto Freyre, *Casa Grande e Senzala* (1933: English trans., *The Masters and the Slaves*, New York, 1946). On Freyre, Peter Burke and Maria Lúcia G. Pallares-Burke, *Gilberto Freyre: Social Theory in the Tropics* (Oxford, 2008).

[11] Marilyn G. Miller, *Rise and Fall of the Cosmic Race: The Cult of 'Mestizaje' in Latin America* (Austin, TX, 2004); Joshua Lund, *The Impure Imagination: Towards a Critical Hybridity in Latin American Writing* (Minneapolis, 2006); In a broader context, cf. Robert J. C. Young, *Colonial Desire: Hybridity in Theory, Culture and Race* (London, 1995).

[12] Steven Feld, 'The Poetics and Politics of Pygmy Pop', in Born and Hesmondhalgh (eds.), *Western Music* 254–79.

[13] Richard Grove, 'The Transfer of Botanical Knowledge between Asia and Europe, 1498–1800', *Journal of the Japan-Netherlands Institute* 3 (1991) 160–76; Grove, 'Indigenous Knowledge and the Significance of South West India for Portuguese and Dutch Constructions of Tropical Nature', *Modern Asian Studies* 30 (1996), 121–44.

[14] Antonio Cornejo Polar, 'Mestizaje and Hybridity: The Risks of Metaphors – Notes' (1997: English trans. in *The Latin American Studies Reader*, ed. Ana Del Sarto, Alicia Ríos and Abril Trigo, Durham, NC, 2004, 760–4); cf. Martin Lienhard, *La voz y su huella: escritura y conflicto étnico-social en América Latina (1492–1988)* (Havana, 1990), 133 and *passim*.

[15] Freyre, *Masters*.

[16] Melville J. Herskovits, 'African Gods and Catholic Saints in New World Negro Belief', *American Anthropologist* 39 (1937), 635–43.

[17] Fernando Ortiz, *Contrapunteo cubano* (1940: English trans., *Cuban Counterpoint: Tobacco and Sugar*, 1947, new edn Durham, NC, 1995); Alejo Carpentier, *La música en Cuba* (1946: English trans., *Music in Cuba*, Minneapolis, 2001).

18 Américo Castro, *España en su historia* (1948: English trans., *The Structure of Spanish History*, Princeton, 1954).

19 Arnold J. Toynbee, *A Study of History*, vol. VIII (London, 1954), 274ff., 472ff., 481ff.

20 Toynbee, *Study*, vol. VIII, 495.

21 Toynbee, *Study*, vol. X, 143.

22 Arnaldo Momigliano, *Alien Wisdom: The Limits of Hellenism* (Cambridge, 1975); Momigliano, *On Pagans, Jews and Christians* (Middletown, CT., 1987); Glynn Bowersock, *Hellenism in Late Antiquity* (Cambridge, 1990).

23 Franz Cumont, *Les religions orientales dans le paganisme romain* (1909: English trans., *Oriental Religions in Roman Paganism*, London, 1911); cf. David Frankfurter, 'Syncretism and the Holy Man in Late Antique Egypt', *Journal of Early Christian Studies* 11 (2003), 339–85.

24 Peter Burke, *The European Renaissance* (Oxford, 1998), introduction.

25 An early example of the ecumenical trend is Jean Delumeau, *Naissance et affirmation de la Réforme* (Paris, 1965). Cf. Thierry Wanegffelen, *Ni Rome ni Genève. Des fidèles entre deux chaires en France au XVIe siècle* (Paris, 1997). Wanegffelen also collaborated in the revised edition of Delumeau's book (Paris, 1997). For a still broader overview, see William Monter, 'Religion and Cultural Exchange, 1400-1700', in Heinz Schilling and István G. Tóth (eds.), *Religion and Cultural Exchange in Europe*, 1400–1700 (Cambridge, 2006), 3–24. On Catholic writers in Protestant England, Jean Orcibal, 'Les spirituels français et espagnols chez John Wesley', *Revue de l'Histoire des Religions* 139 (1951), 50–110; Louis Martz, *The Poetry of Meditation* (New Haven, 1954), 125–35.

26 Gwyn Prins, *The Hidden Hippopotamus: Reappraisal in African History* (Cambridge, 1980); Serge Gruzinski, *La colonisation de*

l'imaginaire (Paris, 1988); Erik Zürcher, 'Jesuit Accommodation and the Chinese Cultural Imperative', in David E. Mungello (ed.), *The Chinese Rites Controversy* (Nettetal, 1994), 31–64.

27 Ronaldo Vainfas, *A heresia dos indios* (São Paulo, 1995); cf. Alida C. Metcalf, 'Millenarian Slaves? The Santidade de Jaguaripe and Slave Resistance in the Americas', *American Historical Review* 104 (1999), 1531–59.

28 Ikuo Higashibaba, *Christianity in Early Modern Japan: Kirishitan Belief and Practice* (Leiden, 2001), especially 29, 35, 38.

29 Fernando Ortiz, 'Los factores humanos de la cubanidad' (1939: rptd in his *Etnia y sociedad*, Havana, 1993, 1–20), at 5.

30 N. A. Yevsina, 'L'viv', in Jane Turner (ed.), *Dictionary of Art*, vol. XIX (London, 1996), 835–7.

31 Henri Terrasse, *Islam d'Espagne: une rencontre de l'Orient et de l'Occident* (Paris, 1958); Ignacio Henares Cuéllar and Rafael López Guzman, *Arquitectura mudéjar granadina* (Granada, 1989); Gonzalo M. Borrás Gualis, *El Islam de Córdoba al Mudéjar* (Madrid, 1990), 191–219. On the Arabic inscription in San Roman, María Rosa Menocal, *Ornament of the World: How Muslims, Jews, and Christians Created a Culture of Tolerance in Medieval Spain* (Boston, 2002), 131.

32 Partha Mitter, *Indian Art* (Oxford, 2001), 87.

33 Mitter, *Indian Art,* 181–2; Gauvin A. Bailey, *The Jesuits and the Great Mogul: Renaissance Art at the Imperial Court of India, 1580–1630* (Washington, DC, 1998).

34 G. Freyre, *Ingleses no Brasil* (1948, new edn Rio de Janeiro, 2000), 223: it is a pity that this pioneering study has never been translated into English. Sharon F. Patton, *Afro-American Art* (Oxford, 1998), 25, 39, 41.

35 Serge Gruzinski, *La pensée métisse* (1999: English trans., *The Mestizo Mind: The Intellectual Dynamics of Colonization and Globalization*, London, 2002).

36 Thomas R. Metcalf, *An Imperial Vision: Indian Architecture and Britain's Raj* (London, 1989), 73–4; Terrasse, *Islam*; William B. Fagg, *Afro-Portuguese Ivories* (London, 1959); Ezio Bassani, 'Gli oliphanti Afro-Portoghesi della Sierra Leone', *Critica d'Arte* 163 (1979), 175–201.

37 Michael Sullivan, *The Meeting of Eastern and Western Art from the Sixteenth Century to the Present Day* (London, 1973), especially 63–4; James Cahill, *The Compelling Image: Nature and Style in Seventeenth-Century Chinese Painting* (Cambridge, MA, 1982), 70–5, 91, 176.

38 Aby Warburg, *Gesammelte Schriften* (1932: English trans., *The Renewal of Pagan Antiquity*, Los Angeles and Oxford 1999); Ernst H. Gombrich, *Art and Illusion: a Study in the Psychology of Pictorial Representation* (London, 1962); Richard L. Gregory, *Eye and Brain: the Psychology of Seeing* (London, 1966).

39 Charles Boxer, *Mary and Misogyny* (London, 1975); Serge Gruzinski, *La guerre des images* (1989: English trans., *Images at War: Mexico from Columbus to Blade Runner (1492–2019)*, Durham, NC, 2001); David A. Brading, *Mexican Phoenix: Our Lady of Guadalupe* (Cambridge, 2002).

40 Peter Burke, *The Fortunes of the Courtier: The European Reception of Castiglione's 'Cortegiano'* (Cambridge, 1995).

41 Angel Rama, *Transculturación narrativa en América Latina* (Mexico, 1982).

42 Rasheed El-Enany, *Naguib Mahfouz: The Pursuit of Meaning* (London, 1993), 17–18.

43 Chantal Zabus, *The African Palimpsest: Indigenization of Language in the West African Europhone Novel* (Amsterdam, 1991).

44 Thomas Brückner, 'Across the Borders: Orality Old and New in the African Novel', in Peter O. Stummer and Christopher Balme (eds.), *Fusion of Cultures?* (Amsterdam and Atlanta, 1996), 153–60; Emmanuel E. Obiechina, *An African Popular Literature*

(Cambridge, 1973); Obiechina, *Culture, Tradition and Society in the West African Novel* (Cambridge, 1975); Robert Mandrou, *De la culture populaire aux 17e et 18e siècles: la bibliothèque bleue de Troyes* (Paris, 1964); Júlio Caro Baroja, *Ensayo sobre la literatura de cordel* (Madrid, 1969).

45 Young, *Postcolonialism*, 338.

46 Roger Bastide, *Les religions africaines au Brésil* (1960: English trans., *The African Religions of Brazil: Toward a Sociology of the Interpenetration of Cultures*, Baltimore, 1978); Renato Ortiz, *A morte branca do feiticeiro negro – Umbanda* (Petrópolis, 1978); Diana DeG. Brown, *Umbanda: Religion and Politics in Urban Brazil* (Ann Arbor, 1986).

47 Herskovits, 'African Gods'; Miguel Barnet, *Cultos afrocubanos* (1995: English trans., *Afro-Cuban Cults*, Princeton, 2001); James T. Houk, *Spirits, Blood, and Drums: The Orisha religion in Trinidad* (Philadelphia, 1995).

48 Maria Laura Viveiros de Castro Cavalcanti, *O mundo invisível: cosmologia, sistema ritual e noção de pessoa no espiritismo* (Rio de Janeiro, 1983); David J. Hess, *Samba in the Night: Spiritism in Brazil* (New York, 1984).

49 Victor L. Oliver, *Caodai Spiritism* (Leiden, 1976).

50 Jean-François Bayart, *L'état en Afrique: la politique du ventre* (Paris, 1989).

51 On Debussy, Mervyn Cooke, 'The East in the West', in Jonathan Bellman (ed.), *The Exotic in Western Music* (Boston, 1998), 258–80; on Roussel and Delage, Jann Pasler, 'Race, Orientalism and Distinction', in Born and Hesmondhalgh (eds.), *Western Music*, 86–118.

52 Jonathan Bellman, 'Indian Resonances in the British Invasion, 1965–1968', in Bellman, *Exotic*, 292–306.

53 Carpentier, *Music in Cuba*; Fernando Ortiz, *Música afro-cubana* (Madrid, 1975), 25.

54 George Lipsitz, *Dangerous Cross-Roads: Popular Music, Postmodernism and the Poetics of Place* (London, 1994), 14–15.

55 Lipsitz, *Dangerous Cross-Roads*, 4, 18.

56 Freyre, *Masters*, 343–9.

57 Peter Burke, *Languages and Communities in Early Modern Europe* (Cambridge, 2004), 111–40.

58 Burke, *Languages and Communities*, 129–30.

59 The film is preserved in the Department of Anthropology, University of Cambridge.

60 Quoted in Alex Bellos, *Futebol: The Brazilian Way of Life* (London, 2002), 35.

61 On the Latin style of football, Archetti, *Masculinities*.

62 Júlio Caro Baroja, *El Carnaval, análsis histórico-cultural* (Madrid, 1965).

63 Peter Burke, 'Carnival in Two Worlds', *Revista de Dialectología y Tradiciones Populares* 51 (1996), 7–18, rpt in his *Varieties of Cultural History* (Cambridge, 1993).

64 Maria Clementina Pereira Cunha, *Ecos da folia: uma história social do carnaval carioca entre 1880 e 1920* (São Paulo, 2001).

65 Stefania Capone, *La quête d'Afrique dans le candomblé* (Paris, 1999).

66 Linda Colley, *Captives* (London, 2002).

67 Said, *Out of Place*; Ang, *On Not Speaking Chinese*.

68 Maxine Hong Kingston, *The Woman Warrior* (New York, 1976); Gloria Anzaldúa, *Borderlands / La Frontera: The New Mestiza* (San Francisco, 1987).

69 Paul Gilroy, *The Black Atlantic* (London, 1993).

70 A collection of studies in Louise B. Tachot and Serge Gruzinski (eds.), *Passeurs culturels: mécanismes de métissage* (Paris, 2001).

71 Natalie Z. Davis, *Women on the Margins: Three Seventeenth-Century Lives* (Cambridge, MA, 1995); Bartholomé Bennasar and Lucille Bennassar, *Les chrétiens d'Allah* (Paris, 1989); Lucetta Scaraffia, *Rinnegati: per una storia dell'identità occidentale* (Rome, 1993).

72 Mercedes García-Arenal and Gerard Wiegers, *Entre el Islam y Occidente* (English trans., *A Man of Three Worlds: Samuel Pallache, a Moroccan Jew in Catholic and Protestant Europe*, Baltimore, 2003).

73 Amin Malouf, *Léon l'Africain* (Paris, 1986); Oumelbanine Zhiri, *L'Afrique au miroir de l'Europe: fortunes de Jean Léon l'Africain à la Renaissance* (Geneva, 1991). See also Natalie Z. Davis, *Trickster Travels: A Sixteenth-Century Muslim Between Worlds* (New York, 2006).

74 One of the few studies of these metaphors is Robert Baron, 'Amalgams and Mosaics, Syncretisms and Reinterpretations: Reading Herskovits and Contemporary Creolists for Metaphors of Creolization', in R. Baron and Ana C. Cara (eds.), 'Creolization', a special issue of *Journal of American Folklore* 116 (2003), 88–115.

75 Clifford Geertz, *Local Knowledge* (New York, 1983).

76 G. W. Pigman III, 'Versions of Imitation in the Renaissance', *Renaissance Quarterly* 33 (1980), 1–32.

77 Maria Lúcia Pallares-Burke, *Nísia Floresta, O Carapuceiro e outros ensaios de tradução cultural* (São Paulo, 1996).

78 Ann Moss, *Printed Commonplace-Books and the Structuring of Renaissance Thought* (Oxford, 1996), 12, 15, 51, etc.

79 Werner Jaeger, *Early Christianity and Greek Paideia* (Cambridge, MA, 1962); Henri de Lubac, *Exegèse médiévale* (1959–64: English trans., *Medieval Exegesis: The Four Senses of Scripture*, 2 vols., Edinburgh, 1998–2000).

80 Michel de Certeau, *L'invention du quotidien* (1980: English trans., *The Practice of Everyday Life*, Berkeley, 1984); Paul Ricoeur, 'Appropriation', in his *Hermeneutics and the Human Sciences*, ed. John B. Thompson (Cambridge, 1983), 182–93. Cf. Peter Burke, 'The Art of Re-Interpretation: Michel de Certeau', *Theoria* 100 (2002), 27–37.

81 Certeau, *L'invention du quotidien*, 292.

82 Oliverio Girondo, 'Manifiesto de Martín Fierro', quoted in Carlos

123

A. Jáuregui, *Canibalia. Canibalismo, calibanismo, antropofagia cultural y consumo en América Latina* (2005: 2nd edn, Madrid, 2008), 427n.

83 Jáuregui, *Canibalia*, 393–460; the quotations, 431, 546.

84 Euclides da Cunha, *Os sertões* (1902: 2 vols., São Paulo, 1983), 140, 237, 249.

85 Fernand Braudel, *La Méditerranée et le monde méditerranéen à l'époque de Philippe II* (1949: English trans., *The Mediterranean and the Mediterranean World*, 2 vols., London, 1972–3); Edward Said, *Culture and Imperialism* (London, 1993).

86 For example, Einar Haugen, 'The Analysis of Linguistic Borrowing' (1950: rptd in his *The Ecology of Language*, Stanford, 1972, 79–109).

87 Alphonse Dupront, *L'acculturazione* (Turin, 1966).

88 Fernando Ortiz, 'El mutuo descubrimiento de dos mundos' (1943: rptd in his *Etnia y sociedad*, 21–7).

89 Peter J. Hugill and D. Bruce Dickson, *The Transfer and Transformation of Ideas and Material Culture* (College Station, TX, 1988). Cf. Michel Espagne and Michael Werner (eds.), *Transferts. Les relations interculturelles dans l'espace franco-allemand 18e et 19e siècles* (Paris, 1988); Rebekka Habermas and Rebekka von Mallinckrodt (eds.) *Interkultureller Transfer und nationale Eigensinn* (Göttingen, 2004).

90 Robert Muchembled (ed.), *Cultural Exchange in Early Modern Europe* (4 vols., Cambridge, 2007).

91 Aby Warburg, 'Austausch künstlerische Kultur zwischen Norden und Süden' (1905: rpt in his *Gesammelte Schriften*, Leipzig, 1932, 179–84).

92 Johannes Bettray, *Die Akkomodationsmethode des Matteo Ricci in China* (Rome, 1955); David Mungello, *Curious Land: Jesuit Accommodation and the Origins of Sinology* (Stuttgart, 1985).

93 George Elison, *Deus Destroyed: The Image of Christianity in Early Modern Japan* (Cambridge, MA, 1973), 54–84.

[94] Pierre Dahmen, *Un jésuite brahme: Robert de Nobili* (Louvain, 1924).

[95] Jacques Gernet, *Chine et christianisme: action et réaction* (Paris, 1982).

[96] Louise M. Burkhart, *The Slippery Earth: Nahua–Christian Moral Dialogue in Sixteenth-Century Mexico* (Tucson, 1989); Amos Megged, *Exporting the Reformation: Local Religion in Early Colonial Mexico* (Leiden, 1996), 5–12.

[97] Anselm Strauss, *Negotiations* (San Francisco, 1978); P. M. Larson, 'Intellectual Engagements and Subaltern Hegemony in the Early History of Malagasy Christianity', *American Historical Review* 102 (1997), 969–1002.

[98] Anthony D. Buckley and Mary C. Kenney, *Negotiating Identity: Rhetoric, Metaphor and Social Drama in Northern Ireland* (Washington, 1995); Jeffrey Lesser, *Negotiating National Identity* (Stanford, 1999).

[99] Anthony Pym, 'Negotiation Theory as an Approach to Translation History: An Inductive Lesson from 15th-Century Castille', in Yves Gambier (ed.), *Translation and Knowledge* (Turku, 1993), 27–39; Umberto Eco, *Mouse or Rat? Translation as Negotiation* (London, 2003).

[100] Gruzinski, *Pensée*, 235, 280.

[101] Burke, *Languages and Communities*.

[102] Peter Bakker and Maarten Mous (eds.), *Mixed Languages* (Amsterdam, 1994).

[103] Mario Carelli, *Carcamanos e comendadores: os italianos de São Paulo da realidade à ficção (1919–1930)* (São Paulo, 1985), especially 52–3, 103–22.

[104] Baron, 'Amalgams and Mosaics'.

[105] Michael Albrecht, *Eklektik: Eine Begriffsgeschichte mit Hinweisen auf die Philosophie- und Wissenschaftsgeschichte* (Stuttgart, 1994).

[106] Cumont, *Oriental Religions*.

[107] Ulrich Berner, *Der Synkretismus-Begriff* (Wiesbaden, 1982);

Charles Stewart and Rosalind Shaw (eds.), *Syncretism/Anti-Syncretism* (London, 1994).

108 Herskovits, 'African Gods'; cf. Andrew Apter, 'Herskovits's Heritage', *Diaspora* 1 (1991), 235–60.

109 Young, *Colonial Desire*.

110 Burke and Pallares-Burke, *Freyre*, 62–3; Bastide, *Religions*.

111 Miller, *Rise and Fall*.

112 Mikhail Bakhtin, *Voprosy literatury; estetiki* (1975: English trans., *The Dialogical Imagination* (Austin, TX, 1981, 80–2, 358–9). Cf. Gary S. Morson and Caryl Emerson, *Mikhail Bakhtin: Creation of a Prosaics* (Stanford, 1990), especially 139–45.

113 Edward Said, *Culture and Imperialism*, xxix; cf. Homi K. Bhabha, *The Location of Culture* (London, 1994), 112–15; Pnina Werbner and Tariq Modood (eds.), *Debating Cultural Hybridity* (London, 1997).

114 Bhabha, *Location*, especially 111–18. On Bhabha, Bart Moore-Gilbert, *Postcolonial Theory* (London, 1997), 114–51.

115 Carl Wilhelm von Sydow, *Selected Papers on Folklore* (Copenhagen, 1948), 11ff., 44ff.

116 Daniel Miller, 'Coca-Cola: A Black Sweet Drink from Trinidad', in Miller (ed.), *Material Cultures* (London, 1998), 169–87.

117 James L. Watson (ed.), *Golden Arches East: McDonald's in East Asia* (Stanford, 1997); Pieterse, *Globalization and Culture*, 49–52.

118 Roland Robertson, 'Globalization or Glocalization?' *Journal of International Communication* 1 (1994), 33–52.

119 Stewart and Shaw (eds.), *Syncretism/Anti-Syncretism*; Sergio F. Ferretti, *Repensando o sincretismo* (São Paulo, 1995); Stephan Palmié, 'Against Syncretism: Africanizing and Cubanizing Discourses in North American Orisa Worship', in Richard Fardon (ed.), *Counterworks* (London, 1995), 73–104; Charles Stewart, 'Syncretism and its Synonyms: Reflections on Cultural Mixture', *Diacritics* 29.3 (1999), 40–62.

120 Young, *Colonial Desire*.

121 Edward E. Evans-Pritchard, *Social Anthropology* (Oxford, 1951), 81–2. Cf. Thomas O. Beidelman (ed.), *The Translation of Cultures* (London, 1971); Talal Asad, 'The Concept of Cultural Translation', in James Clifford and George E. Marcus (eds.), *Writing Culture: The Poetics and Politics of Ethnography* (Berkeley, 1986), 141–64; Gisli Pálsson (ed.), *Beyond Boundaries: Understanding Translation and Anthropological Discourse* (Oxford, 1993); Sanford Budick and Wolfgang Iser (eds.), *The Translatability of Cultures* (Stanford, 1996).

122 Malcolm Crick, *Explorations in Language and Meaning: Towards a Semantic Anthropology* (London, 1976), 164.

123 Pallares-Burke, *Nísia Floresta*; Peter Burke and R. Po-chia Hsia (eds.), *Cultural Translation in Early Modern Europe* (Cambridge, 2007).

124 George Steiner, *After Babel* (London, 1975), 28, 47.

125 Ulrich Berner, *Untersuchungen zur Verwendung des Synkretismus-Begriffes* (Wiesbaden, 1982); James Clifford, *Person and Myth: Maurice Leenhardt in the Melanesian World* (Berkeley, 1982), ch. 5; Jan Assmann, 'The Translation of Gods', in Budick and Iser (eds.), *Translatability*.

126 Herskovits, 'African Gods'.

127 Mary Hunter, 'The Alla Turca Style', in Bellman, *Exotic*, 43–73.

128 Wenchao Li, *Die christliche China-Mission im 17. Jht: Verständnis, Unverständnis, Misverständnis* (Stuttgart, 2000).

129 Laura Bohannan, 'Shakespeare in the Bush' (1966: rptd in David S. Kaston, ed., *Critical Essays on Shakespeare's Hamlet*, New York, 1995, 9–18).

130 Lienhard, *La voz*.

131 Dell Hymes (ed.), *Pidginisation and Creolisation of Languages* (Cambridge, 1971).

132 Peter Bakker and Maarten Mous (eds.), *Mixed Languages*

127

(Amsterdam, 1994); cf. Sarah G. Thomason, *Language Contact* (Edinburgh, 2001), 89–90, 125.

133 Lee Drummond, 'The Cultural Continuum', *Man* 15 (1980), 352–74; there is a good discussion from several points of view in Charles Stewart (ed.), *Creolization: History, Ethnography, Theory* (Walnut Creek, CA, 2007).

134 Ulf Hannerz, 'The World in Creolization', *Africa* 57 (1987), 546–59; Hannerz, 'Centre–Periphery, Creolization and Cosmopolitanism', in Eliezer Ben-Rafael and Yitzhak Sternberg (eds.), *Comparing Modernities: Pluralism versus Homogeneity* (Leiden, 2005), 461–81. A criticism of this approach may be found in Jonathan Friedman, *Cultural Identity and Global Process* (London, 1994), 195–232.

135 Charles Joyner, 'Creolization', in C. R. Wilson and W. Ferris (eds.), *Encyclopaedia of Southern Culture*, Chapel Hill, 1989), 147–9; Ulf Hannerz, *Cultural Complexity* (New York, 1992), 264; David Buisseret and Steven G. Reinhardt (eds.), *Creolization in the Americas* (Arlington, 2000), 19–33; Baron and Cara (eds.), 'Creolization'.

136 José Luis Romero, *LatinoAmérica: las ciudades y las ideas* (1976; 2nd edn, Buenos Aires, 2001), 119–72.

137 Peter Galison, *Image and Logic: A Material Culture of Microphysics* (Chicago, 1997), 47. My thanks to my Cambridge colleague Richard Drayton for bringing this innovative study to my attention.

138 Hymes (ed.), *Pidginisation*, 75–7.

139 Bastide, *Religions*, 365.

140 Roland Barthes, *Système de la mode* (Paris, 1967); Juri Lotman, 'The Poetics of Everyday Behaviour in Russian 18th-Century Culture', translated in Lotman and Boris Uspenskii, *Semiotics of Russian Culture* (Ithaca, 1977), 631–56; Paul Ricoeur, 'The Model of the Text: Meaningful Action Considered as a Text', *Social*

Research 38 (1971), 529–62. Cf. Doris Bachmann-Medick, *Kultur als Text: die anthropologische Wende in der Literaturwissenschaft* (Frankfurt, 1996).

141 Lloyd Rudolph and Susanne Rudolph, *The Modernity of Tradition: Political Development in India* (Chicago, 1967), 11.

142 Jacques Gernet, *Chine et christianisme: action et réaction* (1982: English trans., *China and the Christian Impact: A Conflict of Cultures*, Cambridge, 1985).

143 Nathan Wachtel, *La vision des vaincus* (1973: English trans., *The Vision of the Vanquished: The Spanish Conquest of Peru Through Indian Eyes, 1530–1570*, Hassocks, 1977); Solange Alberro, *Les espagnols dans le Mexique colonial: histoire d'une acculturation* (Paris, 1992).

144 D. C. Dorward, 'Ethnography and Administration: The Study of Anglo-Tiv "Working Misunderstanding"', *Journal of African History* 15 (1974), 457–77; Prins, *Hidden Hippopotamus*; cf. Wyatt MacGaffey, 'Dialogues of the Deaf: Europeans on the Atlantic Coast of Africa', in Stuart Schwartz (ed.), *Implicit Understandings*, ed. (Cambridge, 1994), 249–67.

145 Robert A. Voeks, *Sacred Leaves of Candomblé* (Austin, TX, 1997), 61.

146 Paul C. Johnson, *Secrets, Gossip and Gods: The Transformation of Brazilian Candomblé* (Oxford, 2002), 115.

147 Roger Bastide, 'Le principe de coupure et le comportement afro-brésilien', *Anais xxxi congreso de americanistas* 1 (1954), 493–503.

148 David Pollack, *The Fracture of Meaning: Japan's Synthesis of China from the Eighth through the Eighteenth Centuries* (Princeton, 1986).

149 Mary Louise Pratt, *Imperial Eyes: Travel Writing and Transculturation* (London, 1992).

150 Galison, *Image*, 46, 803.

151 Clara García Ayluardo and Manuel Ramos Medina (eds.), *Ciudades mestizas*, (Mexico City, 2001).

152 Suketu Mehta, *Maximum City: Bombay Lost and Found* (London, 2005), 499.

153 Halil Inalcık, *The Ottoman Empire 1300–1600* (London, 1973), 106–202. Cf. Gernot Heiss and Grete Klingenstein (eds.), *Das Osmanische Reich und Europa, 1683 bis 1789: Konflikt, Entspannung und Austausch* (Vienna, 1983).

154 Terrasse, *Islam*; Henares Cuéllar and López Guzman, *Arquitectura mudéjar*; Borrás Gualis, *El Islam*; Menocal, *Ornament*.

155 Eero K. Neuvonen, *Los arabismos del español en el siglo xiii* (Helsinki, 1941); Samuel M. Stern, *Hispano-Arab Strophic Poetry* (Oxford, 1974); Luce López-Baralt, 'Crónica de la destrucción de un mundo: la literatura aljamiado-morisca', *Bulletin Hispanique* 82 (1980), 16–58.

156 On 'intercultures', Anthony Pym, *Method in Translation History* (Manchester, 1998), 177–92.

157 Edward P. Thompson, *The Making of the English Working Class* (London, 1963); Pierre Bourdieu, *La distinction* (1979: English trans., *Distinction: A Social Critique of the Judgement of Taste*, London, 1984).

158 Norbert Elias, *Studien über die Deutschen* (1989: English trans., *The Germans: Power Struggles and the Development of Habitus in the Nineteenth and Twentieth Centuries*, Cambridge, 1996); Ute Frevert, *Ehrenmänner: Das Duell in der bürgerlichen Gesellschaft* (Munich, 1991).

159 Lynn Hunt, *Politics, Culture and Class in the French Revolution* (Berkeley, 1984); Ross McKibbin, *Classes and Cultures: England 1918–51* (Oxford, 1998).

160 Arturo Graf, *L'anglomania e l'influsso inglese in Italia nel secolo xviii* (Turin, 1911); Freyre, *Ingleses*; Michael Maurer, *Aufklärung und Anglophilie in Deutschland* (Göttingen, 1987).

161 A brief and lucid comparative view can be found in Arnold J. Toynbee, *The World and the West* (London, 1953).

162 Pallares-Burke, *Nísia Floresta*.

163 Gilberto Freyre, *Ordem e progresso* (1959, new edn Rio de Janeiro, 2000), 786; Jeffrey D. Needell, *A Tropical Belle Epoque: Elite Culture and Society in Turn-of-the-Century Rio de Janeiro* (Cambridge, 1987), 166–71; Roberto Schwartz, 'As idéias fora do lugar' (1994: English trans., 'Misplaced Ideas: Literature and Society in Late Nineteenth-Century Brazil', in Schwartz, *Misplaced Ideas: Essays on Brazilian Culture*, ed. John Gledson, London, 1992, 19–32); Elías José Palti, 'The Problem of "Misplaced Ideas" Revisited', *Journal of the History of Ideas* 67 (2006), 149–79.

164 David Nirenberg, *Communities of Violence: Persecution of Minorities in the Middle Ages* (Princeton, 1996). Cf. Menocal, *Ornament*, whose phrase 'a culture of tolerance' in her sub-title risks exaggerating this aspect of medieval Spain, although the author is well aware of conflicts.

165 Braudel, *Mediterranean*.

166 Samuel Collins, *The Present State of Russia* (London, 1671), 67.

167 Sylvie Deswarte, *Il 'perfetto cortegiano' D. Miguel de Silva* (Rome, 1989).

168 On language purification, Burke, *Languages and Communities*, ch. 6.

169 Simon Ottenberg, 'Ibo Receptivity to Change', in William R. Bascom and Melville J. Herskovits (eds.), *Continuity and Change in African Cultures* (Chicago, 1959), 130–43; Harold K. Schneider, 'Pakot Resistance to Change', in the same volume, 144–67.

170 Castro, *Structure*.

171 Donald Keene, *World Within Walls: Japanese Literature of the Pre-Modern Era, 1600–1867* (London, 1976).

172 Francis Robinson, 'Islam and the Impact of Print in South Asia', in Nigel Crook (ed.), *The Transmission of Knowledge in South Asia* (Delhi, 1996), 62–97.

173 Noel Perrin, *Giving up the Gun: Japan's Reversion to the Sword, 1543–1879* (Boston, 1979).

174 Ottenberg, 'Ibo Receptivity to Change'; Schneider 'Pakot Resistance to Change'.

175 Quoted in Anthony Cross, 'Russians on Foreigners', in Simon Franklin and Emma Widdis (eds.), *National Identity in Russian Culture* (Cambridge, 2004), 74–92, at 85.

176 Petr Chaadaev, *Major Works* (Notre Dame, 1969), 32.

177 Da Cunha, *Sertões*, vol. I, 140, 237, 249.

178 Simon Swain, *Hellenism and Empire: Language, Classicism and Power in the Greek World, AD 50–250* (Oxford, 1996), 1–64.

179 Henri Estienne, *Deux dialogues du nouveau langage françois* (1578: ed. Pauline M. Smith, Geneva, 1980).

180 Peter von Polenz, 'Sprachpurismus und Nationalsozialismus', in Eberhard Lämmert (ed.), *Germanistik* (Frankfurt, 1967), 113–65.

181 Serif Mardin, *The Genesis of Young Ottoman Thought* (Princeton, 1962), 115; cf. Joseph R. Levenson, *Liang Chi-Ch'ao and the Mind of Modern China* (Cambridge, MA, 1953).

182 Edward Seidensticker, *Low City, High City: Tokyo from Edo to the Earthquake, 1867–1923* (London, 1983).

183 Freyre, *Ingleses*, 189; Vainfas, *Heresia*, 158.

184 Claude Lévi-Strauss, *La pensée sauvage* (Paris, 1962); Certeau, *L'invention*.

185 John Irwin, 'Origins of the "Oriental Style" in English Decorative Art', *Burlington Magazine* 97 (1955), 106–14.

186 Robert Finlay, 'The Pilgrim Art: The Culture of Porcelain in World History', *Journal of World History* 9 (1998), 141–87, at 177.

187 Sergio Zoli, *La China e la cultura italiana dall '500 al '700* (Bologna, 1973); Madeleine Jarry, *Chinoiserie* (New York, 1981).

188 Peter Burke, *The Fabrication of Louis XIV* (New Haven, 1992).

189 Peter Burke, 'Learned Culture and Popular Culture in Renaissance

Italy', in Maurice Aymard et al. (eds.), *Pauvres et riches: mélanges offerts à Bronislaw Geremek*, (Warsaw, 1992).

190 S. Takashina (ed.), *Paris in Japan: The Japanese Encounter with European Painting* (Tokyo, 1987).

191 John Corbett, 'Experimental Oriental', in Born and Hesmondhalgh (eds.), *Western Music*, 163–86; Arthur Groos, 'Return of the Native: Japan in *Madama Butterfly / Madama Butterfly* in Japan', *Cambridge Opera Journal* 1 (1989), 167–94.

192 Reiko Tsukimura, 'A Comparison of Yeats' *At the Hawk's Well* and its *Noh* Version', *Literature East and West* 11 (1967), 385–97; Richard Taylor, *The Drama of W. B. Yeats: Irish Myth and the Japanese Nō* (New Haven, 1976), 111–20.

193 Bernard Lewis, 'From Babel to Dragomans', *Proceedings of the British Academy* 101 (1999), 37–54.

194 Frances Karttunen, *Between Worlds: Interpreters, Guides and Survivors* (New Brunswick, 1994), 1–22, 114–35; Dejanirah Couto, 'The Role of Interpreters, or *Linguas*, in the Portuguese Empire in the Sixteenth Century' (2001), online, www.brown.edu/Departments/Portuguese_Brazilian_Studies/ejph/html/issue2/html.

195 Peter Burke, 'The Renaissance Translator as Go-Between', in Werner von Koppenfels (ed.), *Renaissance Go-Betweens* (Berlin, 2005), 18–31; on double consciousness, Gilroy, *Atlantic*.

196 John Tedeschi, 'Italian Reformers and the Diffusion of Renaissance Culture', *Sixteenth-Century Journal* 5 (1974), 79–94; Frances Yates, *John Florio* (London, 1934).

197 Roger Bastide, 'Mémoire collective et sociologie du bricolage', *Année Sociologique* (1970), 65–108.

198 Stefania Capone, *La quête d'Afrique dans le candomblé* (Paris, 1999); Sidney M. Greenfield, 'The Reinterpretation of Africa: Convergence and Syncretism in Brazilian candomblé', in Greenfield and André Droogers (eds.), *Reinventing Religions:*

Syncretism and Transformation in Africa and the Americas (Lanham, MD, 2001); Ortiz, *A morte branca*.

199 Edward Relph, *Place and Placelessness* (London, 1976); Joshua Meyrowitz, *No Sense of Place: The Impact of Electronic Media on Social Behaviour* (New York, 1985); Marc Augé, *Non-lieux* (1992: English trans., *Non-Places: Introduction to an Anthropology of Supermodernity,* London, 1995).

200 Emily Apter, 'On Translation in a Global Market', *Public Culture* 13 (2001), 1–12.

201 Ien Ang, *Watching Dallas: Soap Opera and the Melodramatic Imagination* (London, 1985); Tamar Liebes and Elihu Katz, *The Export of Meaning: Cross-Cultural Readings of 'Dallas'* (New York, 1990).

202 Miller, 'Coca-Cola'.

203 Graham Aelred, *Zen Catholicism* (London, 1964); David M. Bader, *Zen Judaism* (New York, 2002).

204 Robert Lafont, *La révolution régionaliste* (Paris, 1967).

205 Sigmund Freud, 'Das Tabu der Virginität' (1918: English trans. in *Complete Psychological Works,* ed. James Strachey, vol. XI, London, 1957, 191–208).

206 Anton Blok, 'The Narcissism of Minor Differences', *European Journal of Social Theory* 1 (1998), 33-56.

207 Anthony Cohen, *The Symbolic Construction of Community* (Chichester, 1985), 50.

208 Charles Ferguson, 'Diglossia', *Word* 15 (1959), 325–40.

209 Cf. James Clifford, *Routes: Travel and Translation in the Late Twentieth Century* (Cambridge, MA, 1997).

210 Toynbee, *Study,* vol. VIII, 498–521.

211 Marshall Sahlins, *Historical Metaphors and Mythical Realities: Structure in the Early History of the Sandwich Islands Kingdom* (Ann Arbor, 1981); Sahlins, *Islands of History* (Chicago, 1985).

212 Hannerz, 'World'; cf. Hannerz, *Complexity*.

134

Index

Index

Index